OUT *in* EVANSVILLE

AN LGBTQ+ HISTORY *of River City*

KELLEY MATTHEW COURES

Published by The History Press
Charleston, SC
www.historypress.com

First published 2023

Manufactured in the United States

ISBN 9781467153874

Library of Congress Control Number: 2022949527

CONTENTS

FOREWORD

I am honored to write the foreword to this book. Kelley has a passion for history and is a master storyteller, revealing truths that many don't know—and possibly don't want to know.

Kelley has played a huge role in my work. As CEO of Leadership Everyone, I have led thousands of community members to envision a better future for our region. Kelley volunteers to present the unvarnished history of our community, highlighting injustices to minorities. His fearless willingness to enlighten helps us all learn from our mistakes to create a more equitable future.

I am so grateful for Kelley's courageous approach to life and for writing this incredible book, which I believe will help readers grow in understanding and hope.

—Lynn Miller Pease
CEO, Leadership Everyone
Evansville, Indiana

On a clear day, rise and look around you and you'll see who you are.
—Alan Jay Lerner

ACKNOWLEDGEMENTS

This book was made possible by the foundations in our community laid by many people who no longer survive. The queer history of any city rests on the memory of those who passed this way but never had their life story told. Friends I dined with, danced with and dreamed with who died in the epidemic are remembered here.

I would like to acknowledge the gifts of time and memories shared by our LGBTQ elders who sat with me or talked on the phone for hours reminiscing about the past. Paul C shared so much history regarding his work in attempting to organize gay life in the 1950s and early 1960s, and in his role as the Dazzling Denise Nichols, he organized gay entertainment when such things were very dangerous. Thanks to Mallory for sharing her memories of coming out as a lesbian in the early 1970s and her stories about Laura Luebbehusen. Thanks to Rachael Evans for memories of Pal's Steak House and contributions of photos, along with Bruce Crowe, who shared lots of photos and stories of the 1980s in Evansville. Thanks to Dick Engbers for stories and references to the 1960s and local theater.

Thanks to Evy Electra, who, by virtue of long-standing friendships in the drag community, has become a keeper of the history in photos and memorabilia of decades of entertainers who made audiences cheer, laugh and cry. Thanks to Mike and Mickey Bradham for sharing their stories of gay life before the modern age. Thanks to Dr. James MacLeod for his advice and help in putting the book together.

Thanks go to Charlene Tolbert for professionally editing and proofreading. I get so caught up in stories I lose track of punctuation. Thanks to JD Opel for information on modern drag shows and expansion of LGBTQ entertainment to largely heterosexual places in Evansville, plus Jessica and Mo for welcoming them. Thanks also to Ann Tornatta for memories of her brother. Thanks to Belinda Breivogel for keeping Miss Ellen's dream alive.

A personal thanks to my friend and mentor Carol McClintock for being a "don't care kind of gal" during a period when there weren't many, plus her husband, Lloyd Winnecke, for being a loyal friend and giving career advice and guidance my entire working life. Thanks to Nancy Drake for helping me develop my writing skills in a commercial format (and plenty of late-night hijinks in gay places). Thanks to Tracy Harbison for being there to listen and help make connections.

Thank you to both Stacey Easley at the AIDS Resource Group of Evansville and Rachel Trout of Matthew 25 for information about your organizations. Many thanks to the members of River City Pride for their tireless work to celebrate our community and the photos of events this past year. I love each of you.

Finally, thanks to my husband, Justin Allan Coures, who at thirty knows more about LGBTQ history than he ever wanted to know, and our two French bulldogs, Rocky and Rambo, who had to wait every night to play until I finished my work for the day. This book is dedicated to Justin because without him my life would be empty.

Any errors in this book are my responsibility and no one else's.

PROLOGUE

DEFINING THIS WORK

Joseph Goebbels, the propaganda minister in Hitler's Third Reich, made an interesting observation during the 1942 Wannsee Conference as Germany developed the "final solution" for European Jewry. Goebbels pointed out that simply killing all the Jews would not erase Judaism. No, he said; you must destroy the Stars of David and the Torah scrolls, burn the synagogues and books and photographs. To erase a culture, you must also destroy its history. If you don't, in four hundred years some student of archaeology will dig up a relic or a photograph and wonder what it was, and the whole thing will start again. Destroy the history and you erase the people forever.

This book is an attempt to preserve the history of people and show the long timeline the LGBTQ+ citizens of Evansville took on their journey from the closet to parades down Main Street.

Before we begin our journey through Evansville, Indiana's past with regard to what we now refer to as the LGBTQ+ community, we should establish what this book is and what it is not. No book nor any work can ever tell the entire, complete history of the community. Too many have passed on without leaving any documentation of their lives. Gay and lesbian, bisexual and transgender people have lived and died in Evansville since its earliest days, but until late in the nineteenth century, there was no written evidence that they were here or that the larger community was aware of us.

For a century, people who became aware of their sexuality or gender identity had to hide that for fear of violence, incarceration and ostracism from community and family. There were no examples of public personalities who presented a positive image to follow, especially after 1895 and other scandals that followed. The term "closet" might have originated here, as it is such an apt expression. Evansville has always been a bastion of religion. Mainline Protestantism and devout Catholicism dominate the faith landscape and taught that being a homosexual was worse than being a leper: you chose this life. Of course, now we know that is not true.

Likewise, what this book is not is a complete recounting of the history of bars in the city vis-à-vis LGBTQ people. There were indeed places other than those mentioned here that were, from time to time, places some queer people gathered to have community (like the Forget Me Not Inn on the east side). Also, this was never intended to be a complete and concise history of drag performers in the city. That is impossible, as there were, over the course of the sixty or so years for which we can find evidence, too many to list. Someone will undoubtedly read this book and declare it incomplete because their favorite wasn't mentioned. I apologize here for the omission.

Over the course of a year, I interviewed a variety of LGBTQ elders who provided a wealth of information, stories, photographs and hearty laughs. I owe them a debt I cannot repay except to acknowledge their gifts.

This book is not a psychoanalytical study of sexuality or the kaleidoscope of the gender spectrum or sexual identity. There is no way I could incorporate even the beginnings of such work. This is not a religious study of humans and their chosen gods either. For some, homosexuality is something one does, not who one is, and therefore is sinful. We bypass that off-ramp as well.

What, then, is this book? Even to some LGBTQ readers, it will be so much froth and little substance because they were not mentioned nor was anyone they knew. Gay politics can be brutal. People who dislike drag as a cultural phenomenon (and there are quite a few gay men who virulently dislike it) will say the chapter devoted to it is a waste. I disagree. I have attempted, to the best of my ability, to document the events, places, personalities and photographs that demonstrate what I consider to be the timeline that shaped both our own cultural identity and the awareness and thoughts of the city at large.

The chapter about AIDS/HIV was particularly painful to write. I served on the board of the AIDS Resource Group for seven years when it was very difficult to raise money and awareness. The years between 1993 and 1999 were difficult, but it was in that mid-'90s period when things began to change for us, and a wide spectrum of community leaders chose to become involved. That made all the difference. I watched quite a few friends die. In one's thirties, that seldom happens outside of wartime or some major natural disaster.

In 2019, a very public celebration of Pride emerged in Evansville. The first Pride parade through the downtown occurred in June, sponsored and organized by a new group, River City Pride, along with a daylong festival at the Haynie's Corner neighborhood, our own Greenwich Village if you will, in the city's art district. The day before, the Art District neighborhood merchant organization hosted street drag performers as part of its First Friday festivities. Thousands of people—a large proportion of them heterosexuals along with their children—cheered and clapped and handed dollars to the performers. These events had been happening in bigger cities for decades, but not here.

This book takes a critical look at the path the LGBTQ community took to reach that moment. Even as we watch some political attempts to further marginalize our transgender loved ones, we must fight for them, for all rights of citizenship are worth fighting for.

This book wasn't easy to write. I hope that the reader looks at this not so much as a parochial story but a universal one that shows that with courage, determination and truth, a marginalized people can gain a place at the table. As Shirley Chisholm said, "If they don't have a seat for you, bring a folding chair."

CHAPTER 1

SEX AND THE VICTORIAN CITY

Evansville, Indiana, is a medium-sized city in the southernmost pocket of the state, on a bend of the Ohio River. Settled in 1812, the city grew rapidly after 1837, when the federal government announced it would build a canal system connecting the Mississippi River to Lake Erie. The terminus of one part of the canal would be in Evansville. This announcement led to a rapid rise in population and industry, a great migration of Germanic people and building wealth for some families.

There was a wharf at the foot of what became Main Street, and riverboats, both passenger and freight, stopped there to load and unload every day of the week, giving employment to both white men and freedmen who'd come across the Ohio seeking liberty before the Civil War and after the war during the Black diaspora from the Deep South.

The blocks lining the river, along what was known as Water Street, were for many decades lined with taverns and "houses of ill fame" that deckhands and other roughnecks frequented. The newspapers of those days are littered with stories of gunfights, fisticuffs and loose women. In January 1864, a Black minister was stabbed to death outside a saloon by young men on a spree. The one who did the killing was released by a Union army police officer. There was little in the way of law enforcement on the waterfront. Gradually, city fathers tried to confine the sex trade to an area just west of what was becoming the main business district into a "tenderloin" area known as High Street.

This small area was less than three blocks long, a maze of crooked streets and Victorian houses and commercial buildings, mainly rooming houses and saloons. Roustabouts and rivermen would go from tavern to tavern along Water Street, eventually "doing the line" (visiting multiple places) at the bordellos or *bagnios* (brothels) along and around High Street.

Many of the properties were owned by prominent men in the city and rented to smart, savvy women who operated the houses. These were tough women who fought not only one another but also men and law enforcement when they felt encroached upon. In some cases, the madams, as they were called, would also look out for one another and cooperate to stop predators and those who would exploit underage girls for profit. This was long before the Mann Act of the 1920s, which criminalized taking a woman across state lines for the purposes of prostitution.

A good example of Evansville's madams, Nell Evans lived in and operated a "resort," as the Evansville newspapers referred to it, at 1 Walker Street at its intersection with High Street. It was, according to media of the day, the only house in good condition with a manicured lawn. Evans once said, "Evansville's finest have come through these doors, men that is." The house was built by a prominent businessman whose wife refused to occupy it due to its location. He reportedly sold it to Evans in the early 1900s at a very low price and visited the house often.

Evans operated her house of ill fame under the watchful eyes of law enforcement and city administrations until her death in 1949. She bequeathed the home to one of her most loyal employees, who had worked for her for decades. Evans's family sued to break the will, but a local judge upheld it, and the woman took ownership. The house was demolished along with the rest of the area in 1960.

One of the most notorious of the tenderloin's taverns stood on First Street at Clark, near the segregated high school for Black students. The address of the saloon was 333 Upper First, but habitués just called it the "three Treys." Several times a month, there would be a stabbing or other fight, usually over a woman or gambling losses, as illegal gaming happened upstairs.

From the 1880s until the "district," as it was known, was shut down during World War II, the tenderloin flourished with reputed payments to police and administrations that campaigned on the promise to "clear the sin district" but then realized its value. Police patrolled the area but did not enforce anti-prostitution laws. They simply kept the violence at a minimum and arrested any underage visitors or sex workers.

In 1919, the city, under Mayor Benjamin Bosse, opened the first venereal disease clinic near the fashionable McCurdy Hotel on First Street near Locust. Administrations saw to it that the women who worked in the district were examined regularly and received treatment if found to have been infected with one or more diseases. It became known that the city on the Ohio River had the only government-supported prostitution district in the country.

A scandal involving two policemen and the administration of Mayor Frank Griese in 1932 almost spelled the end of the party on High Street, but Griese lost the next election, and the investigation into "protection payments" ended.

The thought at the time, according to the "obituary" written about the district as the entire neighborhood faced a wrecking ball in the name of urban renewal, was that the law enforcement of the day felt that keeping all of the vice in one area was easier to manage than if it was widespread in the city, as it later became. It was in this environment—a bifurcated political disposition to vice yet with a Victorian attitude about sex in general—that the first references to homosexuality are found.[1]

A roundup of criminal convictions appeared in the January 6, 1887 *Evansville Courier* showing the following adjudicated cases of sex "crimes" in 1886:

Adultery	*6*
Prostitution	*75*
Patronizing a prostitute	*20*
Visiting a brothel	*5*
Keeping a "house of Ill fame"	*22*
Sodomy	*1*

Evansville had an uneasy relationship with sex. Publicly, polite society turned its head and didn't look at what was happening in the tenderloin, just as white citizens turned their heads from the severe economic and social deprivations foisted on its African American citizens during this period. White middle-class God-fearing churchgoing Evansville refused to accept what it did not understand.

It was in 1895, during this heyday of sex and scandal, that Evansville came face to face with homosexuality in the person of Oscar Wilde, a locally popular author from Great Britain. The April 1895 trial of Wilde on charges of gross indecency and sodomy with young men at a London male brothel owned by his friend Alfred Taylor prompted much conversation in Evansville, as his works were very popular. After his conviction and sentence to two years' hard labor by the British court, his books were pulled from the shelves in schools and libraries around the nation and Evansville.[2]

The editor of the *Evansville Journal* wrote on his conviction:

> *Among the good things that have come from the bench are the words used by the judge in London, in sentencing Oscar Wilde and his partner in debauchery, Alfred Taylor, which are worthy of remembering. Such a descent from decency as was developed in the case of these two men could hardly be imagined in a civilized community and much less in the instance of the man Wilde who essayed to lead the world to higher aspirations with his pen. Such a disgusting mess has not been brought to the public notice in years and it is hoped it is the last.*[3]

An *Evansville Courier* editorial expressed what was probably the opinion of the day in the city about the desired end of anyone who lived as Wilde did: "Nothing is wanted to make the downfall of Oscar Wilde as degraded as the human mind can conceive. The public decree against him will be pitiless and inexorable. It is difficult to see what refuge there is for him except that which Brutus sought."[4] Of course, in Shakespeare's *Julius Caesar*, Brutus dies by suicide. And for generations, the public reflected back on Wilde's scandal and indeed may have believed suicide was the cure. It happened a lot.

The fear of homosexuality led to the State of Indiana passing a law in 1881 outlawing "unnatural" sex acts, defined as any act that could not result in procreation and specifically between two of the same sex. It was not removed from the state criminal code until 1977, when only "forced acts" were retained as criminal. The Victorian attitudes prevailed for ninety-six years in a city that not only permitted but also entertained newspaper readers with scandalous stories and occasional humor about a neighborhood of brothels. The difference was that Evansville's brothels employed women who served the sexual appetites of men.[5]

The first major scandal in the local media involving homosexuality and sodomy occurred in 1922, when four men and one woman were arrested and charged with sodomy and abetting sodomy. Benny Young, a twenty-two-year-old owner of a taxi company, and Pearl Money, nineteen, were convicted of "instigating sodomy" with Herman Schucker. Two other taxi drivers participating in the sex party, Charles Huber and James Williams, were convicted of public indecency. In this case, the issue of cunnilingus was ruled to also be covered by the law. It seems the Roaring Twenties in Evansville were off to a scandalous start. Young appealed his conviction. The appeal took several years to reach the state supreme court, which in 1927 upheld his conviction. One jurist, a former prosecutor named George

OSCAR WILDE DYING A PAUPER

Man Who Has Achieved International Notoriety Sick and Destitute in a Paris Hospital

PARIS, France, Oct. 24.—Oscar Wilde the poet and playwright, is sick and destitute in a hospital in this city. Saturday he submitted to a surgical operation that may cost his life. In the event of his recovery to the extent that he can stand the fatigue of travel he will be taken to Scotland, where friends have offered him a home.

OSCAR WILDE.

After his losing conflict with the English courts Wilde made his home in this city. He hoped to rebuild his shattered fortunes, but the fates were against him and he encountered many hardships. He struggled along until he reached the point of absolute destitution, and then sickness came upon him.

Friends of former days sought him out and kept him alive by charities, and finally sent him to the Hospital la Salpetriere when it was learned that he must undergo an operation.

Wilde was born in Dublin in 1856 and was educated at Trinity college in that city. He went to London in 1879 and originated the aesthetic movement, which was satirized by Gilbert in the opera of "Patience," written for music composed by Sir Arthur Sullivan. In 1881 he visited America and delivered 200 lectures on art. From 1880 to 1895 he was busy with his pen and turned out several volumes of poems, essays and novels. He is the author of numerous plays, many of which have been produced in America.

In 1893 Wilde wrote a one-act tragedy which he entitled "Salome." The play dealt with biblical history, as is suggested by the title, and its production in London was prohibited by the lord chamberlain because of its alleged irreverence. On account of this prohibition the author announced his intention of becoming a citizen of France. "Sa-

Evansville Courier, October 25, 1900, on the death of Oscar Wilde. All of his works were pulled from U.S. schools and the library after his 1895 show trial in England. *Evansville Vanderburgh Public Library*.

Heilman, singled out Vanderburgh County as "the jurisdiction that defined prosecution of sodomy cases in the US."[6]

In addition to the anti-sodomy law, Indiana had outlawed miscegenation (race mixing) in its 1851 constitution. Those laws were not removed until 1965. There were several convictions in Vanderburgh County under those laws as well. This area permitted sex for sale but outlawed sex that it didn't like.

Through the 1930s and 1940s, there were numerous arrests and convictions of consenting male adults who were caught in entrapment situations or by bad luck. In the Sunset Park area near the riverfront, there are numerous cases documented. Many times, such charges were made worse for the accused, as their entire societal identity became part of the story. For example, in 1948, Phillip Henderson, forty-one, and Private Thomas LeMasters, twenty-seven, of Camp Breckinridge in Kentucky, were arrested in Sunset Park. An *Evansville Press* article gave both men's addresses and identified Henderson as a post office employee.[7]

In 1952, three men were arrested on "morals" charges: Charles James, a twenty-six-year-old hairdresser; Vernon Carlson, a forty-six-year-old accountant; and Captain Andrew Bailey, twenty-seven, a soldier from Kentucky. The article, of course, gave the home address of each man and listed Fort Campbell for the unfortunate soldier. They were all arrested at Sunset Park. The *Press* article stated that the three arrests represented a new police "drive on sexual perverts in the city."[8]

In December 1939, the *Evansville Courier* reported an entire group of African American men was arrested for sodomy along with several underage Black youths. The men were convicted and sent to the Indiana State Penitentiary for two to fourteen years. The sixteen-to-eighteen-year-old youths were all sentenced to two to fifteen years at the Indiana Reformatory. All the men's addresses were listed in the article, as were the addresses of the Black youths. Their race was prominently mentioned as well.[9]

Through the decades of the 1940s and 1950s, numerous other cases against men were filed in Evansville Circuit Court, and in almost all of them, the men were convicted and sent to prison. For some lucky men, their prison sentence was suspended if they agreed to leave the city permanently, but their lives had been laid bare. Notably, some of those charged were servicemen who were sent back to either Fort Campbell or Camp Breckenridge. We assume the military dealt with them harshly as well.

It was not until after World War II that the civilized world began looking at homosexuality differently. Psychologists and social reformers who wrote syndicated columns in daily newspapers began taking on the issue and trying, badly, to explain it to the general public. It was an effort to move the attitudes from that of criminal deviation to one more explainable in psychiatric terms: homosexuality was—incorrectly of course—described as a curable illness.

CHAPTER 2

DEAR DOCTOR

It was rare to read about homosexuality before the 1940s in Evansville newspapers. As we have seen, arrests and convictions for "morals charges" were the only way the city approached the subject for the first decades of the twentieth century (and beyond really until liberation). However, the daily newspapers began carrying columns written by syndicated authors, presumably licensed physicians and psychologists, when the "analysis" fad took hold in America after the Great Depression. Films and radio programs featured comics poking fun mostly at women for taking to the couch and spilling their innermost thoughts to a psychiatric professional when they couldn't work through their problems on their own.

These syndicated doctors would generally respond to letters submitted by "patients" asking general questions that could be answered in a few columns of newsprint, thus giving an answer that might apply generally to a wide audience with a similar problem.

Beginning in 1937, Dr. George W. Crane of Northwestern University first wrote about female homosexuality in response to an October 26 letter from a man wondering why a girl he liked wouldn't pay any attention to him but constantly fastened her affection on a female friend. Dr. Crane responded in his "Diagnosis" section that the woman in question was stuck in a childhood devotion to her own sex. The doctor advised him that she could be made to evolve to a "normal" affection for the opposite sex, but the transition is difficult. He advised the man to encourage her to seek professional help to free herself from "childish affections."[10]

In a September 29, 1938 column, Dr. Crane told his readers about Vera, a woman just out of college who continued to live with a roommate. He wrote that the two women "kiss and hug and are sentimental towards each other to the point of nausea." The doctor again explained that poor Vera was arrested by inadequate emotional development. He said that 90 percent of the American population were trained to look on such people as lepers, but they are so caught up in their devotion to each other they cannot see the pain they cause their loved ones.[11]

In a September 1941 column, Dr. Crane addressed the shame a young man felt in admitting he was having homosexual liaisons with "vulgar type men." He related stories about his parents, who would have violent arguments in their home, his father occasionally brandishing a pistol. The young man told the doctor in his letter he had vowed never to marry and had fallen into homosexuality by "accident." The doctor told him in his diagnosis that most homosexual men are the result of just such a troubled upbringing, and if they could face the issues with their fathers head on and work through them, their homosexuality would fade away like the phase that it was.[12]

Whether or not readers fully accepted these "case studies," there formed a general attitude among many Evansville residents at the time that homosexuality could very well not only be an illness but also could be cured, but it did not stop the criminal charges therein.

Dr. Crane, in a 1943 column, reported to his readers that in his opinion, mannish girls with short haircuts and who wore slacks were probably responsible for the growing trend of male homosexuals because if a man "wants to date a man he won't go for a substitute; he wants the real thing." Also, "fat girls should avoid flowered fabrics, banish belts and square-necked frocks. Abolish cross stripes and only wear vertical styles." The doctor was also apparently a fashion advisor.[13]

Dr. Crane discussed male homosexual teachers as preferring girl students, as they were less boisterous in classes.[14]

The big news in Evansville, as in the rest of the country in November 1947, was the release of the Kinsey Report. Alfred Kinsey, the sex researcher from Indiana University, released his study of American men, which turned a bright light onto the prevalence of homosexual behavior in American men. Kinsey reported that nearly 20 to 40 percent of all men—far more prevalent than previously thought—reported some same-sex activity in their sexual past. The release of the Kinsey report and its publication in the local paper elicited several outraged letters to the editor complaining that such "news" did not belong in a family newspaper, as it caused questions from young people that parents were not prepared to answer.

Pink Scare

As the 1950s dawned in Evansville, the city was inundated by the same fear of communism as the rest of the nation. The McCarthy hearings were followed closely by local newspaper readers and TV viewers once there was a television broadcast station near enough for clear reception. Along with rooting out communism, the fanatical sifting out of homosexuals from the federal government was a prime concern in Evansville.

When ninety-one homosexuals were terminated from the U.S. State Department, the editor of the *Evansville Press* expressed the paper's delight in the action but criticized the Truman administration nonetheless. Wrote the editor on March 17, 1950:

> *Now that the appropriate Senate subcommittee has interested itself in the subject they should go further and learn how so many perverts happened to congregate in the State department to begin with, how many of them remained on the payroll and for how long after their abnormalities were discovered and who was responsible. The taint is not removed by just getting rid of the queers. The public confidence will not be restored until the officials responsible are given the boot. There may be some jobs that can be handled effectively by persons with abnormal sex habits but not in the diplomatic service or any agency entrusted with our security. It is true not only because of their emotional instability but also because the practices of such people make them an easy target for blackmail by enemy agents.*[15]

An early figure in the history of transgender people was Christine Jorgensen, the recipient of one of the first sex reassignment surgeries in Denmark. George Jorgensen was a doctor and father in New York who flew to Europe and returned as a woman. She was a minor celebrity for a while. Local newspapers ran flattering photos of Christine, although some readers thought them in poor taste. Later, the *Courier* ran many "help" columns from featured writer Dear Abby, who had struck up a friendship with Christine Jorgensen and would solicit from her helpful advice she could give those questioning their gender in letters to her column.[16]

The Evansville Police Department followed the trend in major cities, "cracking down" on gay men by hiding in places where they were known to congregate: Sunset Park, Main Street between 2nd and 3rd Streets late at night, Mesker Park on the west end. Arrests increased for those caught up in sting operations against men "cruising" in those areas. The 1950s and early 1960s were dangerous in Evansville for gay men who ventured out to meet one another. There are numerous news accounts of men arrested on "morals charges" or "sodomy charges" in the Evansville newspapers. Men were also frequently arrested at the Union Depot on Fulton Avenue near Riverside. The Greyhound bus terminal on 3rd Street across from the declining Vendome Hotel was also a favorite hideout for undercover police waiting to catch men meeting in the restrooms or outside the terminal. Sunset Park, which was much larger before the Evansville Museum was built on half of the grounds in 1958–59, was another target of late-night cruising and arrests and the most popular area to meet others. There are numerous accounts of Camp Breckenridge and Fort Campbell soldiers arrested for sodomy in Evansville from the time of World War II until the early 1960s. The soldiers often picked up young men near the bus station on Third Street who turned out to be under the age of eighteen, leading to more serious charges.

A frequent name in the newspapers during this period was Rudolph Ziemer, the co-owner of a funeral home. He was arrested several times between 1946 and 1952 for having sex with men. His last arrest resulted in his checking himself into a St. Louis hospital to "treat" his homosexuality. Another sensational story of the time is the still unsolved murder of an attractive young man, who might have been the first major LGBTQ murder that drew national attention here. Many clues seem to suggest he was a victim of a hate crime.[17]

CHAPTER 3

ANDREW REAGAN

1954

Rogers Dam on the Muskegon River near Osceola, Michigan, is one of the oldest hydroelectric dams in the nation. The current below the dam is swift and the river treacherous to boaters, but the area draws many fishermen. In late March 1960, a party of fishermen was casting lines from shore when they spotted what appeared to be an automobile submerged in the swift, swirling waters. They reported the location to the Michigan State Police, who sent a team of skin divers to examine the vehicle. They found that it was empty of any human cargo.[18]

It took three days for a wrecker crew fighting the current of the Muskegon River and a two-hundred-foot incline up the shoreline to extract the three-thousand-pound automobile, which had apparently been in the water a long time. It was a 1954 black-and-cream Chevrolet. The seats, glove compartment and spare tire had been removed, but the tires on the car were still inflated. The odometer recorded only 4,600 miles—not counting the two-hundred-foot cliff it had apparently been pushed over into the water below.

Michigan police in nearby Reed City traced the ownership of the car back to Evansville, Indiana, by the serial number on the motor block (the license plate was gone) and to one of the strangest murder mysteries to that time. Michigan police requested copies of the file on the killing of twenty-seven-year-old Andrew Reagan, who was murdered in September 1954 and his car stolen by the probable killer or killers. One of the oddities of the case was a cache of letters Reagan had in his apartment from males from all over the country.[19]

Michigan police talked to more than thirty men in the Detroit area who had corresponded with Reagan in the years 1953 and 1954. There was even one man who had traveled to Evansville to visit Reagan several months before his death. The detectives decided all of the men they questioned either had solid alibis or could not be traced to having been in Evansville in September 1954. The case was as dead as Reagan.[20]

MAN, ABOUT TOWN

The Audubon Apartments on SE Riverside Drive in the 1950s was an upscale place to live in the near downtown area. Built in 1914, the three-story tapestry brick building has small balconies for some dwellers and tiny balconettes for others. In the early 1950s, single men with good jobs lived there, including Andrew Reagan, a twenty-seven-year-old terminal manager from the BB & I Trucking Company. Andy, as his friends called him, stood only five feet four inches tall and wore thick-soled black dress shoes that added a little bit of height and maybe some confidence.

A native of Mount Vernon, Kentucky, Reagan had worked for the shipping company for several months, having been promoted to manager of the Evansville terminal in 1954. He had established a small coterie of friends in the city with whom he shared his passions for jazz and fine food and drink. Friends said that he was always impeccably dressed from head to toe. There was never a hair out of place, and he was by all accounts a happy-go-lucky man about town. He wore only one ring, his Glasgow, Kentucky high school class ring made of gold, class of 1947. The jeweler had made a mistake though. Reagan's father had ordered the ring, and the jeweler mistakenly engraved the dad's initials inside the band: "J.D.R." Reagan refused to have his dad's initials changed.

On the evening of Wednesday, September 22, 1954, Reagan left his office at 5:00 p.m. wearing a smart blue suit. He got into his brand-new car, a '54 Chevrolet coupe that was black with a cream top, an unusual custom design that stood out and always drew compliments. He kept the car meticulously clean. Still in his blue work suit, Reagan met his boss, Howard Ownley, for dinner. Ownley had come to town from the Bloomington, Indiana office to meet with Evansville staff that week. The bartender at the Lamplight Inn, a restaurant then located on SE Second Street, a block off Main, recalled

Reagan having a quiet, pleasant conversation over dinner with the other man and said they left about 8:45 p.m. Ownley said Reagan told him he was going home to bed.

Later in the evening, another group of friends met Reagan at the Coral Room, a bar inside the upscale Hotel McCurdy at First Street and Locust near the riverfront. The Coral Room was the stylish cocktail bar where Evansville's "smart set" went to see and be seen. Usually, a live jazz band was playing, and there was a smallish dance floor just off the immense, indirectly lit signature circular mirrored bar that stood in the center of the room. The walls were painted a coral pink, giving the bar its name.

Reagan had apparently gone to his apartment and changed clothes because he was wearing gray slacks and a gray sport jacket with a white shirt and black squared-knit tie when he entered the Coral Room. Friends who were with him said they had some cocktails and socialized until just before midnight, when Reagan bid them a good night and left. He was not seen again after exiting the bar through the main hotel lobby and out the revolving door into the night.

Missing

Reagan was always the first man at work at the BB&I Freight transfer station offices. On Wednesday morning, September 23, workers coming into the office first noticed the parking space usually occupied by Reagan's conspicuous Chevy was empty. Workers entering the office were concerned that he was not at his desk at 9:00 a.m.

Evelyn Hirsch, his secretary, began calling Andy's phone at his apartment, thinking perhaps he had overslept or taken ill. After some time, she went to the office of Arthur Vaughn, the office manager, and alerted him that Andy hadn't shown up (it was after 10:00 a.m.) and she was very worried. Vaughn and his wife were also social friends of Reagan's. Mrs. Vaughn especially fretted that Andy didn't have a girlfriend and was probably surprised he wasn't married at twenty-seven. She had fixed him up with a blind date once that didn't turn out well, apparently.

Vaughn put on his jacket and drove to the Audubon. There was no answer at the door, and Reagan's car was nowhere in sight. Circling back to the office, Vaughn telephoned long distance to Reagan's parents' home in Kentucky. "No," his dad said, they hadn't seen him for several weeks, his last visit being an August Sunday for church and supper. His dad asked

Vaughn to contact the police. Vaughn met the police at the apartment. They managed to get the lock undone on the apartment door with a tool. Nothing was out of place; all of Reagan's personal effects were there, including an overnight bag. Vaughn noted when he got back to the office that Andy's shaving items were still in the bathroom. Andy was always clean-shaven and smelled of aftershave.

That afternoon, Evansville police put out a bulletin to watch for Reagan's car, the black-and-cream 1954 Chevrolet with Kentucky license plate number 28-133. He failed to show up on Friday, September 24, to collect his paycheck. His dad confirmed that Andy had no bank account, so he probably had less than $100 with him at any time that week.

His parents contacted their friend, Kentucky circuit judge J.C. Carter, who along with the parents offered a reward of $500 for information leading to the location of their son. Police on both sides of the Ohio River were becoming convinced Andrew Reagan had been the victim of foul play, although there was no apparent reason. He had no known enemies. Not one person interviewed had anything negative to say about the affable, good-looking young man except that he was sensitive about his height and wore those thick-soled black shoes to look a little taller.[21]

For nearly a week, police watched for signs of Reagan in both Indiana and Kentucky. Police searched his apartment for clues. Detectives found a cache of letters, carefully preserved. Pen pal/mail forwarding services were a popular way for gay people to communicate in the sexually repressive 1950s. The letters, they said, were from men all over the country. The police started sending letters out to some of the men with whom he had corresponded. There were no replies.[22]

Odor

On the warm afternoon of October 1, 1954, a crew of farm laborers was plowing up fields on the farm of James C. Ellis, the wealthy owner of the Dade Park racetrack, which stood along Highway 41 just north of Henderson, Kentucky, the city immediately to the south of Evansville. The men walking behind the giant tractor were approaching the fence along KY State Road 60 where a motorist had reported part of the fence had been flattened and was open. The men looked at each other as they approached the highway as a horrific odor filled their nostrils at the same time. A dead cow, one thought.

THE EVANSVILLE COURIER

109TH YEAR FINAL EDITION EVANSVILLE, INDIANA, SATURDAY MORNING, OCTOBER 2, 1954 SIXTEEN PAGES PRICE FIVE CENTS

Hoosier Political Report

TRUCKING EXECUTIVE FOUND SLAIN

New York Takes Third Straight, 6-2

Gomez Gives Only 4 Hits For Victory

Indians Rest Last Hope Today On Bob Lemon

Weekend Shortage Of Water Expected

France Balks, Drops Wrench In Arms Talks

Mendes-France Insists On Tight Rein On Germany

Andrew Reagan Dumped in Field At Henderson

Decomposed, Badly Beaten Body Of Missing Manager Discovered By Hands on James Ellis Farm

Capt. Birk Harl, Det. Sgt. J. Y. Crawford and Det. Sgt. Charles Basham search Reagan's blood-stained coat. (Staff Photos by Adkins)

Contractor, 40, Fined $300 In Schoolboy Traffic Death

Attorney Gets Senate Seat

Ernest Brown Fills McCarran's Post

Miss Evelyn Hirsch, New Green River Road, and Mrs. Joann Vaughn, 2506 N. Sherman Ave., look at a ring found on Reagan's body in an attempt to identify it.

Evansville Courier, October 2, 1954. Murder victim Andy Reagan's body was found on James C. Ellis's farm near Henderson, Kentucky. *Evansville Vanderburgh Public Library*.

In a drainage ditch next to the fence line where the fence was down, they saw a man's body in a state of decomposition, covered in flies and other insects. His white shirt was almost soaked through with dried blood. The man's head was caved in on one side. He was dressed in gray slacks. About ten feet away, near the fence, was a gray sport coat. The man's shirt was torn at the sleeve and ripped nearly halfway from the body. There had been a struggle.[23]

Henderson County sheriff's officers responded quickly after the call. Sheriff Lee Williams and Coroner Fred Tapp (who also owned the local funeral home) determined the body had been thrown over the barbed-wire fence after death and the sport coat thrown over afterward. Death had come to the man by way of blows to the head, presumably from a tire iron. There were nine holes in the skull, the fatal blow having crushed the left temple bones into the brain.

The coroner said whoever killed the man had continued to crush the skull at least four times after he was dead. The first blow was between the shoulder blades directly to the back, which probably stunned him. He must have bled profusely, Tapp said, because blood had even stained the man's undershorts beneath his outer clothing. Sheriff Williams said in his opinion this was a "crime of passion, not robbery." No wallet or identification was found on the body.[24]

Suspecting it was Andrew Reagan, Tapp called the elder Reagans to come to the morgue. The father was able to identify the unrecognizable body as his only son by a gold Glasgow High School class of 1947 ring he was wearing. The initials inside the band: J.D.R.

CLUES

The young adult set in Evansville was shaken by the screaming headline in the October 2, 1954 *Evansville Press*: "Trucking Executive Found Slain."

In the first week of October 1954, friends and acquaintances of Andy Reagan were questioned several times by detectives from both Indiana and Kentucky. The FBI was called in to look at the case since the presumed abduction and murder crossed a state line. There was very little to go on aside from the stack of correspondence from men around the nation, some of whom had never met Andy but had only written back and forth to him. The contents of the letters were never revealed, as there was no public discussion of the messages they may have contained.

In Reagan's pockets, detectives found only three items: a small pink comb, a black handkerchief and a matchbook. The matchbook was the first solid lead in the case. It was from a fine dining establishment just outside Henderson, Kentucky, about a half mile from the spot Reagan's bloody corpse was discovered. It was called the Montgomery Tea Room on Old Spottsville Road. The yellow brick house with a green-tiled roof was built in 1913 by a man named Baskett, who lost his fortune in the 1920s and reportedly died by suicide by leaping from the roof.

The Tea Room was an ornate Victorian home converted into a genteel dining establishment. Its elegant setting had seen many bridal luncheons and wealthy debutante dinners over the years. Tearooms had a special connotation in queer culture of the 1950s. The owner, Judith Montgomery, sat with detectives in her dimly lit dining room under a crystal chandelier and talked about Andy, whom she knew as a regular customer. She said indeed, he had just been in her place several Sundays for brunch before he disappeared. "He was here several times with the same man, but I didn't know who he was," she told the detectives. "He was taller than Andy, but not as stocky." The two men had been meeting there regularly, but he never introduced himself, nor did Reagan introduce him to her. Detectives reported in their notes that Montgomery was fond of Andy because in her mind he resembled her favorite movie actor, James Stewart. Police found little table markers in Reagan's apartment from the Tea Room, perhaps taken as souvenirs to remember a special moment or conversation.

Digging deeper into the immediate state of mind of Reagan, detectives interviewed various casual friends of his, mainly those who had seen him that last night. These friends painted a different picture, after the body was found, of the happy-go-lucky businessman they had initially described. They said Andy had a darker side, some depression, they feared, and he had been drinking heavily on weekends, usually traveling out of town to do so. He had damaged the front bumper of his brand-new car shortly after buying it, one friend said. He was distraught over it for a few days and probably had been drunk when it happened. A shop had managed to straighten it out mostly, and it didn't look too bad, but it wasn't perfect, and Andy liked everything to be perfect.

He had no bank account that they knew of, they told police. He seemed to live well but paycheck to paycheck. He would not have had much cash on him the night he disappeared because he would not have received his $110 paycheck ($1,200 in 2021 dollars) until Friday, September 24.

Detectives traveled to nearby cities where Reagan had "pen pals" and interviewed men in Louisville, Nashville and St. Louis, but no one had seen or met with him for months before his death. Clues and names came and went, but nothing turned up any solid evidence. The unusual automobile that Reagan had sported around town had not been seen, other than in rumor. (Two GIs reportedly were offered a ride by a man who looked like Reagan the night of his disappearance, but the driver was too drunk, so they passed him by.)[25]

There were two other stories reported by two separate families in the Henderson, Kentucky area that at the time were discounted by the police.

After the murder was reported, a farmer and his wife told police that on the evening of September 23, 1954, they were sitting on their porch after dark when they spotted a man staggering along their road, which led to Highway 60, toward them. The man was short, wearing a gray jacket and was covered in blood. He reeked of whiskey. In a scratchy voice, he offered them twenty dollars to drive him to Evansville. He told them someone had beaten him and stolen his car and he needed to get home. The farmer told him no and to leave their yard. The man staggered on down the road until they could no longer see him. A few yards down the same road, a mother and her adult daughter were outside and saw the same man staggering down the road toward them, although he did not speak to them. After he disappeared awhile later, they said a new black-and-cream car came speeding by them, but they didn't see the man again. None of the four could identify Reagan from photographs.[26]

Michigan

It was just a few days after the April 1960 discovery of the 1954 black-and-cream Chevrolet at the bottom of the Muskegon River near Reed City, Michigan, that detectives were sure they were on to a solution to the murder of Andrew Reagan. After sending to Henderson, Kentucky, for copies of all the evidence collected in the murder investigation, the Michigan homicide unit found letters addressed to Reagan from a man who lived in Detroit. After five hours of questioning, police released him. Although he admitted he knew Reagan and had traveled to Evansville to meet him, the last time he was in Evansville with Reagan was in May 1954, four months before the murder. The man gave detectives his own list of men who also knew Reagan who still lived in Michigan or had moved back to Kentucky.[27]

The Kentucky State Police fulfilled a public records request by this author that revealed one homosexual relationship Andrew apparently had with a Michigan man named Irwin. Police found in Reagan's apartment a letter dated August 29, 1953, that detailed a weekend spent with Irwin in which Irwin profusely thanked Reagan and cautioned, as a long-distance lover would, "Well dear my eyes are closing….You be good [underlined] understand with me here and you there, there's no way of keeping tab so I will just say be good and let it go at that. Thinking of you…" Irwin begged Reagan to set up another rendezvous as soon as possible, maybe meeting in Cincinnati or Owensboro.

Michigan State Police detectives contacted James Irwin in 1960 after Reagan's car was found and interviewed him about the relationship. The transcript of the interview was included in the documents provided by the public records request, and Irwin detailed his relationship with Reagan and other men. He stated in the sworn statement that he had met Reagan when they both lived in Bloomington, Indiana. in February 1952 and carried on an on-again, off-again romantic relationship through May 1953. Irwin said that Reagan moved to Danville, Illinois, and then Evansville but periodically visited him.

However, Irwin met another man, Albert Ellis, then in the U.S. Army, through a "Correspondence Club" about that same time and established a stronger relationship with him. Ellis and Irwin made plans to live together after Ellis got out of the army and would begin college at Indiana University. Irwin told detectives he cut off the relationship with Andy Reagan at that time, which apparently made Reagan upset, as he was not ready to end the relationship with Irwin. In the letter found in Andy's apartment, Irwin mentioned he hadn't spoken to Albert since the week before (the rest of the sentence was obscured).

In another letter not provided but detailed in the detectives' interview, Irwin mentioned a final letter he got from Andy Reagan in February 1954, seven months before the murder. He said Andy wanted to clear the air. Irwin told the detectives, "He said he finally understood my character, that I had no emotional attachment to any men I was with, that I didn't think anymore of Albert than I did of him, that it all made sense and he finally understood my character." Irwin stated he did not answer that letter. Irwin learned of the killing of his former lover when he was called by Kentucky State Police after his information was found in Andy's apartment in the letters and in Andy's personal phone book.

The detectives asked why Irwin was so quick to end his affair with Reagan. Irwin told them he thought Reagan's personal choices were of a "low character" and that he met men in bars for sexual relations and he considered that a "step beneath." Irwin said his opinion was this type of activity might have resulted in Reagan's ultimate fate.

In a demeaning entry, detectives told Irwin that this murder should discourage him from this "homosexual life" and he should see a psychiatrist to try to move himself into a more normal life.[28]

All the investigators over a five-year period who searched for Andrew Reagan's killer knew only one thing for sure: whoever disposed of the car had to be keenly familiar with the remotest geography of the area near the dam. The road to the cliff where the car must have been pushed off is narrow and only accessible by a near-invisible turnoff. The road itself was gravel and difficult to maneuver, but the killer, somehow led by the desire to destroy the last remaining piece of Andrew Reagan's young life, got his prize possession up there and hurled it into the river below.

CHAPTER 4

JACK BURDETTE AND THE YMCA

1960

Evansville, like most cities in America, was anxious on November 3, 1960, as the national election between John F. Kennedy and Richard Nixon was concluding the following week. Local political chatter was mainly about clearing out the High Street slum area that had for one hundred years been the official red-light district and the displacement of its very poor residents. Some of the madams had already relocated their operations to the Haynie's Corner area at the southeast corner of the near downtown where Parrett Street meets Second Street at a weird angle due to the original layout of the city.

In the downtown at Fifth and Vine Streets stands the brick and Indiana limestone five-story YMCA. Designed by Clifford Shopbell, a renowned architect of the nineteenth and early twentieth centuries, the stately U-shaped building was completed in 1914. Originally a segregated facility, the Y catered to a white all-male clientele, split between older influential city gentlemen, well connected and powerful, and an underclass of young men, many of whom drifted into and out of Evansville depending on their obtaining employment and what used to be called "the main chance."

Most of the upper floors of the building were small, individual sleeping rooms that could be rented for a nominal fee on a daily or weekly basis. Young drifters who landed in the city and who had no acquaintances could stay there for a tiny fee or, in some dire conditions, no fee as long as they agreed to do some labor such as janitorial work. As it was a Christian operation, no one was turned away for monetary reasons, only by race for several decades. Earlier in the century, Black men had their own smaller, less-equipped YMCA on the other side of downtown for about twenty years, though it was financially supported by the main Y.

The Y was one of the places homosexual men could find one another for sex. The showers were reportedly one of the most popular cruising areas in town, and many men who rented the small sleeping rooms did so to facilitate sexual liaisons. There is no documentation of such activity, only anecdotal evidence related by conversations with gay elders. Such was the case of Jack Burdette, who actually lived at 426 Adams Avenue in Evansville with his mother, Effie, but who occasionally rented a room at the Y and apparently took a bottle of liquor with him.

Burdette was thirty-six and an Evansville native. His father, Ralph, was a city policeman in Evansville before he retired in the 1940s. Burdette was a popular student at both Centennial Grade School and Reitz High School, appearing in a number of theatrical plays and musical shows during his high school years. He went into the U.S. Marine Corps in 1943 after graduation and served through World War II, reaching the rank of corporal. When he came home, he worked a variety of factory jobs, the last one with Servel Inc., at one time the city's largest industrial employer. In addition, the veteran of the South Pacific war theater also participated in the Community Players, a local drama group.[29] Servel announced its closure in late 1957 and began massive layoffs shortly after, including Jack Burdette.

Burdette was still out of work on the very early morning of November 3, 1960, when, shortly after midnight, he checked into a small fourth-floor room on the Vine Street side of the YMCA. What ensued in the next three hours is shrouded by time. He and another man apparently engaged in sex, and Burdette ended up dead, having been thrown or fallen from the window of his sleeping room. A surviving gay elder was staying in the building at the time and remembered the event as though it was yesterday.

Loud Voices and Breaking Glass

Across Vine Street from the YMCA stands the seven-floor 1930 Art Deco Indiana Bell telephone company building, designed by Kurt Vonnegut Sr. In 1960, there were three shifts of call-switching workers connecting local callers to long-distance or other phone-operating systems not on the Bell network. Operator Lloyd Brinkler was sitting at his call board near the fourth-story window that looked directly across the street into the Y.

Shortly after 3:00 a.m., he heard a loud crash and breaking glass outside. When he looked, in the glare of a streetlight on the sidewalk a man was lying facedown, wearing only a pair of boxer-type underwear and covered in blood and broken glass. Brinkler looked up and saw that the window of the YMCA across from him was broken out and torn Venetian blinds moved in and out of the gaping window. He could see movement inside the room, but with no light, it was just shadows. Brinkler immediately dialed the Evansville Police Department to report what he thought was a suicide. The police station in those days was at Third Street and Walnut, barely six blocks away. Police cars and an ambulance arrived in minutes. Police sergeant Bennett Kellams, the first on the scene, found a faint pulse in the victim. Kellams noted that Burdette's mouth appeared to stuffed with material from a piece of clothing, maybe a shirt. Ambulance attendants loaded Burdette into the vehicle and sped away to nearby Welborn Baptist Hospital, where he died of his injuries less than an hour later. The pathology report showed he could have succumbed to any one of several injuries resulting from a four-story fall to solid concrete.[30]

Back at the YMCA, police detectives were busy rounding up all of the men who were present in the building as residents or working. On the fourth floor, a tall twenty-one-year-old with tousled dark hair identified himself as James Duncan Holcombe from Spartanburg, South Carolina, who had been recently discharged from the U.S. Navy. He had come to Evansville, he said, to find work. He had a small job at the downtown Jerry's Market and was living at the Y. He told police he didn't know anything about the situation.

Another man occupying the room next to Burdette's, Anthony Hawkins, was at first reluctant to talk but later said he heard loud male voices from the room, one an older man and the other who sounded like Holcombe, whom he had talked to several times. Hawkins said at around 3:00 a.m., he was awakened by sounds of a fight and then heard breaking glass. He said that he was hesitant to talk to police, as he was AWOL from Fort Benning, Georgia, but then decided to tell what he knew and go back to the army and face the consequences.

Police then zeroed in on young Mr. Holcombe, who confessed that he had indeed been in Burdette's room and did push him out of the window. He told the police that he had never met Burdette before but that about 2:00 a.m., Burdette knocked on his door and asked him if he wanted to come to his room for drinks. Burdette said that he had some whiskey left over from a party. Holcombe said he was wearing only underwear, but at the Y, that wasn't unusual.[31]

The Evansville Press

Served by United Press International, Scripps-Howard Leased Wire, NEA Service, Science Service and United Press International Telephoto

FINAL HOME EDITION

PRICE SEVEN CENTS

55TH YEAR, NO. 107 EVANSVILLE, INDIANA, THURSDAY, NOVEMBER 3, 1960 68 PAGES

Tax Rates More Than Estimates

Schools Area Up 4 Cents; Hike Elsewhere 2 Cents

By FRED SIEVERS

Official property tax rates payable in 1961 for Vanderburgh County were received here today from the State Tax Board.

The new rates are up from previous tentative rates by four cents for townships located within the Evansville School Corporation and two cents for all other townships.

2 Are Held in Fatal Four-Story Plunge

Victim Falls From Window at 'Y'

By LARRY HAMMERSTEIN

Two men are being held in the death of Jack Burdette, 36, who plunged through a fourth-floor window of the YMCA to the sidewalk below early today.

Burdette, who lived at 426 Adams, died a short time later at Welborn Baptist Hospital, apparently of injuries suffered in the fall.

The dotted line shows where Jack Burdette, 36, of 426 Adams, plunged to his death from a fourth-floor YMCA window to the Vine Street sidewalk early today.

BULLETIN

Urges Compromise

DR. NENNEKER

Dr. Nenneker, Dentist Here 32 Years, Dies

Cancer Is Blamed for Death of Active Sports Fan, Hunter and Civic Leader

Dr. Charles J. Nenneker, 55, Evansville dentist, avid hunter and sports fan, died at 6:30 this morning in Deaconess Hospital.

Where They Are Today

Nixon Off to Texas; Kennedy Heads East

INSIDE THE PRESS

Kennedy TV Film 'Rigged,' Says GOP

Bets Illegal in LV But It's Jack 9-5

Scattered Frost Tonight

Satellite Put In Ionosphere

Undecided Voter, One Out of Six, Will Decide Vanderburgh Vote

Kennedy Holds Edge In Persons Polled

By ROBERT FLYNN

FLYNN

DONALD GLASER

Two Americans Win Nobel Science Prizes

Burglar Gets Reduced Charge

Evansville Press, November 4, 1960. Jack Burdette was thrown from a fourth-story window by James Duncan Holcombe after a sexual encounter. *Evansville Vanderburgh Public Library.*

Holcombe went across the hall to Burdette's room, where they drank for a bit, and then Burdette asked to perform oral sex on him. Holcombe said he allowed it, but once it was over, he wanted to leave the room. Burdette, he told police, would not let him leave. Holcombe was younger and stronger (he had been a welterweight boxer in the navy). He put Burdette in a choke hold, tore some pieces of a shirt that was lying on the small bed, stuffed them in Burdette's mouth and dragged him to the window above a steam radiator. He slammed Burdette's head into the radiator and then pushed him through the glass window. Holcombe admitted he knew Burdette was still alive when he went out the window to his near-certain death.[32]

Holcombe was arrested and charged with second-degree murder. Hawkins got his wish, and Military Police picked him up at the police station that afternoon.[33]

Howard Sandusky

Holcombe got hold of his parents in South Carolina, who immediately drove to Evansville. They hired Howard Sandusky as their son's attorney. Sandusky was a powerful local figure for many years, being involved heavily in Republican politics and running for judge unsuccessfully in the mid-1960s. He and his wife were noted in the society section of the newspapers for decades, serving at various Southern Baptist church events and other charities. Sandusky met with Holcombe and his parents and informed them privately that he had a strategy for their son. It began with changing his confession statement.

A few days after his charge, Holcombe asked to add to his original statement. Police detectives met with him and Sandusky. Holcombe had already stated that Burdette had come to his door, invited him across the hall for drinks and performed a sex act on him, which led Holcombe to push Burdette out the window after stuffing his mouth with the sleeves of a gray striped shirt. To this statement, Holcombe added that after the first sex act was completed, Burdette began asking for another sex act, which Holcombe refused and at that point got up from the bed to leave. Now he said this was when Burdette physically attempted the second sex act, and Holcombe fought him, resulting in Burdette falling through the window during their altercation.

Sandusky was planning a self-defense argument, with a homosexual twist that he thought a jury might buy.[34]

Judge Ollie Reeves was the jurist selected for the Holcombe trial, which got underway with jury selection the first week of March 1961. Each juror was asked this question by Sandusky: "Does a man have a right to defend himself against a homosexual attack the same way a woman does?" The prosecutor never objected to the question. After two days of jury selection, the trial began on March 14, 1961, with a jury of six women and six men.

Holcombe's mother returned to Evansville to sit with the now very clean-cut, neatly dressed defendant, who, according to newspaper stories at the time, never showed the slightest case of nerves, calmly smiling at both his mother and jurors.

Witnesses told of the night of November 3, about the sounds they heard and the sight of Burdette lying facedown on the sidewalk. The coroner stated it was the fall that killed Jack Burdette, but he noted that significant bruising about the mouth and face were definitely not caused by the fall but by blows. The police sergeant testified he saw Burdette's mouth stuffed with cloth. The coroner said there were two pieces of cloth, each roughly twelve by fifteen inches, from the same article of clothing, a gray striped shirt, stuffed nearly all the way into the mouth and upper throat of the victim, who therefore would have been unable to call for help or even speak.

Prosecutor O.H. Roberts painted a picture of a young man ashamed of what he had done, who, in his self-anger, took revenge on Burdette, making sure that he could not cry out for help and sending him plunging fifty feet to his death on a city sidewalk.

Sandusky called only one witness, the defendant himself. Tall and lanky and somewhat uncomfortable being the center of attention, Holcombe told his version of the events. He said Burdette tried to get him drunk, and he allowed Burdette the one sexual act in order to get out of the room. When Burdette demanded another sexual act, he decided he had to knock Burdette out to escape. Holcombe said he used his boxing training to restrain Burdette. He tore the sleeves from a shirt on his bed and stuffed them into Burdette's mouth to keep him quiet. "There's been some robberies in the building, and I didn't want anyone to think I was robbing him," said Holcombe, looking at the jury. "I was trying to hit his head against that radiator to knock him out, but he tried to get out of my hold and whirled around and fell out of the window that was partially open." Holcombe said he didn't know what to do, so he went back to his room.

Sandusky appealed to the jury that this very young navy veteran was only trying to defend himself from a pervert and a second attack on his body, and he had a right to do so, "just like a woman has the right to defend herself against such attacks from men." Sandusky looked at each female juror while making that statement.[35]

It worked.

At about 8:00 p.m. on Friday, March 17, the jury returned a verdict of not guilty. The morning paper showed a smiling Sandusky, a relieved mother and a tall James Holcombe exiting the courtroom. Holcombe said he was

Weather
THE EVANSVILLE COURIER
Final Home Edition

116TH YEAR—NO. 61 EVANSVILLE, IND., SATURDAY MORNING, MARCH 18, 1961 16 PAGES PRICE SEVEN CENTS

Boxer Freed In Fatal 'Y' Plunge

Coroner Reports Drowning Of Jockey's Wife Accident

Slinker Held Blameless In Death

Probe Indicated Husband Driving, Sheriff Reports

Time Testimony: Sheriff Gresham Grim displays a clock found in the car in which Mrs. Mary Elizabeth Slinker drowned. The clock's hands were stopped at 2:02, apparently the time that the car plunged into Ohio River backwaters early Sunday morning. The clock started running again after being allowed to dry. Grim displays the clock in front of a panel of news pictures used in investigating the drowning.

Jobless Dips 2nd Week In a Row

But Total Still Called New High For Time of Year

Cleared In Slaying: James Duncan Holcombe, 22, of Spartanburg, S. C., leaves Circuit Court in high spirits after being found not guilty of second-degree murder. He walks down the corridor with his attorney, Howard Sandusky, (right) and a friend, Janice Killebrew of 622 East Chandler Avenue.

Jury Studies Burdette Case 5 Hours

Holcombe's Mother Weeps Happily As Panel Reports

U.S. Military, Arms Aid to Laos Increased

Tornadoes Rip South

Snow Blankets Texas Panhandle

Rusk, Gromyko Set Meeting for Today

Administration Hopes Session May Ease Cold War Tensions

Evansville Courier, March 18, 1961. James Holcombe is acquitted of murder in the death of Jack Burdette after admitting the crime. *Evansville Vanderburgh Public Library.*

returning to Spartanburg with his mother and twin sister, who had also traveled here for the trial. He did return to South Carolina, but less than a month later, he was back in Evansville.[36]

On April 8, 1961, Holcombe was again living at the Y but also sharing a house at 622 East Chandler with another man, Robert Killebrew. Holcombe had registered under an assumed name at the Y. Killebrew reported to police that his wallet had been stolen by Holcombe the night before while he was sleeping. Police tracked Holcombe to the Y and arrested him while he was using a pay phone. Killebrew's wallet was in his pocket with no cash showing. Unknown to Holcombe, the wallet had a secret compartment where Killebrew kept two ten-dollar bills with writing on them. When police checked the wallet, there they were.

Holcombe ended up serving some prison time after all, serving ninety days at the state penal farm for petit larceny. Theft of a wallet carried a greater weight than murdering a man.[37] Holcombe died in Spartanburg in June 1994 at the age of fifty-five.

CHAPTER 5

RUDOLPH SEVERIN ZIEMER

1963

March 12, 1963, was an unusually warm day in Evansville, Indiana, for early spring. At midday, the temperature had reached seventy degrees. At the Ross Theater on the East Side, the film *Days of Wine and Roses* had been playing to packed audiences all week, and downtown department stores were trumpeting spring dollar days sales. The morning *Courier* reported the Ohio River would crest above flood stage at forty-four feet, and many roads were closed at the levee.

Sometime that evening, Rudolph Ziemer, fifty-six-year-old co-owner of the Ziemer funeral home, backed his 1962 Dodge station wagon out of the long driveway from the home he shared with his sisters Elizabeth and Agnes, also partners in his business, plus a brother, George, a priest, and drove out for the evening. He had a long and unpleasant history with driving in his hometown.

In 1939, he was speeding while intoxicated, crossed the center line on Riverside Drive that curved at what was then Emmett Street near downtown and seriously injured several people in an oncoming vehicle. Lawsuits were filed but settled out of court. Through the 1940s and early 1950s, several other accidents were blamed on his drunkenness, including a motorboat accident on the Ohio Riverfront that was witnessed by several pedestrians along the area overlooking the plaza where boats were launched.[38]

At one time, he had been partners with his older brother, Theodore. Both had graduated from the Askins Embalming Academy in Bloomington, Indiana, which was then affiliated with Indiana University, and opened a funeral home in 1927 in their mother's home on First Avenue in the urban northside neighborhood where they had grown up. In 1935, the business moved into a much larger home once owned by a former mayor, Benjamin Bosse. That opening was advertised in the local press as a major event in the mortuary business, said to be state-of-the-art, with "every convenience to the bereaved."

The brothers split in 1953 with great acrimony over money, and Theodore opened his own mortuary as Fountain Terrace, as he was unable to use the family name. The Ziemer sisters, Elizabeth and Agnes, remained with Rudolph, and together they lived in a sprawling white brick ranch on then suburban outer Lincoln Avenue at Vann Avenue, in an area of stylish and upper-middle-class homes.

No one knows all of the destinations Ziemer had that fateful Tuesday evening in March, but he ended up pulling into the parking lot of the Old Kentucky Barbeque restaurant and bar on South Kentucky Avenue about 9:30 p.m. Kentucky Avenue at that time was U.S. Highway 41 through the city, a busy thoroughfare dotted with eateries and motels from the northern city limit to the state line just south of Riverside Drive. Warning signs had been posted south of there, as the Ohio River had reached flood stage and some roads had been washed out. Most were closed at the point of the levee.

A waitress at the bar later testified that Ziemer, a frequent customer, entered and sat at the bar to order a drink but was already very inebriated. Arnold Jewells, the bartender, served Ziemer a glass of water, as he was coughing, but would not serve him alcohol. Later, Jewells would state in court that he frequently saw Ziemer there with young men, buying them drinks. The waitress had not heard everything but said Ziemer made some remark to a table of young men nearby that led to a shouting match and insults from two of the four. The manager ordered the youths to leave, and they went out into the parking lot.

She said Ziemer got up and staggered outside. She saw him trying to unlock his car door, but two of the four men took his keys from him, and one got in the driver's door after pushing Ziemer into the middle of the front seat. The other man got in the passenger door. The others got into another vehicle, and both cars disappeared into the night. She never saw them again.

Ziemer's sisters became concerned the following day, Wednesday, March 13, when their brother failed to come home. As that day passed into evening without any word, the sisters called the police. The *Evansville Press*, the daily afternoon paper, reported in its March 14 edition that Rudolph

Ziemer was missing and hadn't been seen since Tuesday night at the Old Kentucky Barbeque.

Police were led by a tip to the edge of Weinbach Avenue, a north–south major city street that was closed at that time south of Riverside Drive due to high water. There, about ten feet east of the roadway, they found Ziemer's station wagon fully submerged, the transmission in drive, in the swirling floodwaters. His body was in the front seat lying prone across the bench seat. His face was bruised. His eyeglasses were on the floor of the car, and his necktie had been pulled tightly around his throat, as if having been pulled from behind. A later autopsy showed he had drowned. His lungs were filled with river water, and his face had numerous contusions and many cuts inside his mouth.

Returning to the waitress at the bar where Ziemer was last seen, detectives were told the young men who left in Rudolph's car were paratroopers from Fort Campbell, an army base in Kentucky down Highway 41.[39]

Out on a Spree

That warm March 12 evening was a siren song to several young ladies and their dates. Carol Sue Gentry was twenty years old and single. About 6:30 p.m., she drove her car to the home of her friend Melvina Shutt, and together they ended up at Hamilton's Drive-In, a popular burger joint on Kentucky Avenue, where they met a couple of other girls and a group of soldiers on leave who were hanging out there looking for some fun.

Carol and Melvina left her car and got into a convertible with the top down. With them were two girls she did not know plus four paratroopers. They were Patrick Pirrie, twenty-one; William Thompson, twenty-five; Robert Graymont, twenty-two; and Fred Easton, twenty-two. Carol had dated Graymont before and was glad to see him again. In the crowded car, off they went to the Farmer's Daughter drive-in restaurant up the highway, where the other girls got out to go home.

Graymont was driving. When he pulled out of the drive-in parking lot, he attempted to make a U-turn but ran the convertible off into a ditch. The soldiers got out and tried to get the car back on the road, but they had been drinking and couldn't get the stubborn vehicle free. The girls, still game for fun, told the men they would go back to Melvina's house and get some money and continue the evening. The men stayed to try to free the car from the ditch.

The girls walked back to Hamilton's, where they got back in Carol's car and went home to get more money. When they got back to Kentucky Avenue about thirty minutes later, they found the convertible was still in the ditch, but the GIs were gone. The girls drove up and down the Kentucky Avenue strip until Melvina spotted the GIs in the parking lot of the Old Kentucky Barbeque near the intersection of Riverside Drive. Pulling into the lot, Carol watched as Pirrie and Thompson were struggling with an older man who was apparently very drunk, trying to get him into a white station wagon. They were talking to him, but she didn't recognize him, nor could she hear what they were saying.

After a few minutes, Graymont and Easton got into her car, where Easton passed out in the back seat. Graymont sat in the front between the two girls. Once Pirrie and Thompson were secure in the strange man's car, Thompson, who was driving, motioned for them to follow. Both cars exited the nearly deserted parking lot and drove east on Riverside Drive.

Fingerprints

The two cars—Ziemer's station wagon and Carol's car—drove around the neighborhood near the highway for about a half hour. Carol noticed that Graymont wasn't talking much, nor was Melvina. Both girls were nervous about the circumstances they found themselves in.

Soon, the travelers found themselves at a dead end on Marshall Avenue in the middle of an apartment complex known as Colonial Manor, townhouses with small front yards dotted with children's toys and bicycles. The station wagon stopped, and so did Carol. Suddenly, she saw the overhead light in Ziemer's car go on, and she could see the two GIs hitting the passenger. One after another blow struck his head. It looked as if Thompson had hold of something, maybe the man's tie. Then the light went out again.

After a long while, Pirrie and Thompson got out of the station wagon, ran to Carol's car and got in the back with the unconscious Easton. They were excited and out of breath. Pirrie told them they had "rolled" the old man in the wagon. He had the man's wallet that identified him as Rudolph Ziemer, but to their disappointment, there was no cash in it. Carol began driving aimlessly through the streets as the men discussed their situation.

"We have to go back," said Pirrie. "Our fingerprints are all over the car and that wallet." Graymont said they had to go back to the station wagon and "fix things." She turned around and headed back to the dead-end street where they had left Ziemer and his vehicle.

Wet

Carol's headlights hit the white station wagon, and to her horror, Ziemer appeared to have tried to exit the car. The door was ajar, and his head and shoulder were lying on the pavement. The entire group (except the sleeping Easton) took a vote and decided to take the car to the levee. Pirrie and Thompson jumped out of her car and got Ziemer back into the wagon. The two GIs got back in, and Graymont told her to follow them.

They turned onto Weinbach Avenue at Riverside and headed south to the levee, which rose up like a smooth mountain range along the riverbank circling the city's southside. Built by the U.S. Army Corps of Engineers after the disastrous 1937 flood, it protected Evansville from flooding, as it was doing in March 1963. Weinbach was closed to traffic at this point, but the soldiers got out and moved the barricade and motioned for Carol to follow. Once both vehicles had cleared the levee mound, Carol could see the waters of the Ohio covering the road in front of her.

Graymont got out, went around and moved Carol over. He wheeled her car around facing the opposite direction and told her and Melvina to "stay here and don't turn around." He got out and got in the wagon with Pirrie and Thompson. Easton was snoring.

Carol did turn around, though, and looked back in time to see the red taillights of Ziemer's wagon illuminating water as the front of his car was now half submerged in the shimmering, swollen Ohio River. All three men climbed the levee hill back to Carol's car. Pirrie and Graymont were dry, but Thompson was completely wet from his waist down, having been four feet deep in the floodwaters. They told her they had wiped down everything they could to remove fingerprints. Graymont said the old man was still alive the last time they saw him. They had left the engine running and the gear shift in drive.

The panic was receding from the little group, and they decided to head to Melvina's friend's apartment downtown. Kay Goble invited them in—it was nearing midnight—and all agreed it best never to discuss what had happened during the evening. They had a few drinks at Kay's apartment and listened to records. The men asked Carol to drive them back to get Graymont's car out of the ditch by using a rope and pulling it out with her car, which they did. Carol then dropped Melvina off at her house and went home herself.[40]

A Tip

The Evansville Police had started a search for Ziemer's car on March 14 after his sisters called in the missing person's report that morning. An anonymous tip said they should look near the Weinbach section of the levee. By the time city police headed in that direction, Vanderburgh County sheriff's deputies were already at the levee and had found Ziemer's wallet and personal papers scattered around the water's edge. Officers from both the county and city gathered on the levee. Once they were high enough, they could see the radio aerial of a vehicle submerged in the waters and called for Indiana State Police divers, who arrived on the scene fairly quickly and pulled Ziemer's body from his car. A winch truck was hooked up to the white Dodge wagon and pulled it from its watery resting place that afternoon.

Once word got to the radio and TV stations that Ziemer had been found dead in the river, calls started coming in to detectives, the most important one from a waitress at the Old Kentucky Barbeque who said she had seen Ziemer and four paratroopers arguing and then leaving together Tuesday night from the bar and that they were from Fort Campbell. It was a quick trip to Kentucky to interview the commanding officer, who identified the four who had been on leave to come to Evansville.

The four were gathered together for detectives to interview separately, and immediately Thompson admitted he had beaten Ziemer. Thompson volunteered that he and Pirrie had gotten into Ziemer's car with him and that Ziemer had made "immoral advances" to them both. He said he beat him into near unconsciousness and then got his wallet, but there was no money in it.

He said the trio took Ziemer's car to the levee and pushed it there partly into the floodwaters and then left, but he insisted Ziemer was alive when they left him. Pirrie and Graymont made no statements but admitted they had been present in Ziemer's car. At Fort Campbell, the detectives agreed Easton, who had since recovered, was not involved in the incident. Taking the three back to Evansville, police also charged Carol Gentry and Melvina Shutt as material witnesses but left them free on their own recognizance. The three men were booked and held pending a pathology report.[41]

In the *Evansville Press*, the newspaper began reporting what would eventually be the defense's argument for acquittal. In the report on the arrest and apparent confession of Thompson, the article stated, "Court records show that three times in the last 17 years Ziemer had been arrested

The Evansville Press

Served by United Press International, Scripps-Howard Leased Wire, NEA Service, Science Service and United Press International Telephoto

FINAL HOME EDITION ★ ★ ★ ★ ★ PRICE SEVEN CENTS

57TH YEAR, NO. 221 — EVANSVILLE, IND., FRIDAY, MARCH 15, 1963 — 24 PAGES

Investigators crowded around the 1962 station wagon containing the body of funeral director Rudolph S. Ziemer as the vehicle was pulled from Ohio River backwater by a wrecker near the South Weinbach Avenue levee. The body was discovered yesterday, two days after the 56-year-old man had been reported missing. [Photo by Bill Lemneck]

3 GIs Charged In Ziemer Case; Beating Alleged

FLOOD WATER
ZIEMER'S CAR
BILLBOARD
FENCE
GRAVEL LANE
125 YARDS
WEINBACH AVE
LEVEE
LEVEE

Map shows area where the body of Rudolph Ziemer was found.

Soldier Relates Story to Officials

BULLETIN

Three Fort Campbell, Ky., paratroopers were charged today with assault and battery with intent to rob Rudolph S. Ziemer who was found dead yesterday. Charged in an affidavit signed by Vanderburgh County Sheriff Gresham Grim are Sergt. William Thompson, Specialist Fourth Class Patrick D. Pirrie and Private First Class Robert C. Graymont.

A Fort Campbell, Ky., Army sergeant has told how he beat Evansville funeral director Rudolph S. Ziemer here Tuesday night and then drove the car containing the unconscious mortician into Ohio River backwaters, officials said today.

Veteran Attorney Isidor Kahn Dies Unexpectedly at Age 76

ISIDOR KAHN

Redistricting Bill Vetoed

Action by Welsh Not Unexpected

Teacher Who Left God Out of Oath Defended

River To Begin Falling Slowly Tomorrow

INSIDE THE PRESS

Bridge Book To Be Offered

Lett's Sentence Is Commuted

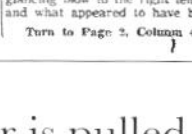

Student Gets 2 Years In Theft of Painting

RUDOLPH ZIEMER

Evansville Press, March 15, 1963. Missing funeral home operator Rudolph Ziemer is pulled from the Ohio River after being beaten by three paratroopers. *Evansville Vanderburgh Public Library.*

for alleged unnatural sexual relations. None of the cases that originated in 1946, 1948 and 1952 resulted in a conviction but on one occasion he had admitted himself to a St. Louis hospital for treatment."

Trial

Pirrie, Graymont and Thompson were not natives of this area. All three called their families to help them with the situation. All three were booked but released on bond. Their parents hired separate attorneys to represent each of them. Howard Sandusky, the attorney who had represented James Duncan Holcombe in his 1961 trial for murdering Jack Burdette, was hired by Pirrie's parents, and Thompson was represented by James Lopp Sr.

On July 2, Circuit Judge Owen Williams set bond at $10,000 for each of the three defendants. All were able to post bond and return to Fort Campbell, where the media reported they "had an excellent service record." Judge Williams admonished them to refrain from consuming alcohol while awaiting their jury trial. Prosecutor O.H. Roberts had asked for $20,000 bond, but to defend that request, he would have had to reveal almost his entire case against them. He agreed to the $10,000.[42]

The original trial date of February 14, 1964, was delayed several times, and finally the case was referred to the next county, Warrick, as pre-trial publicity was seen as a hindrance to the case in Evansville. Vanderburgh County remanded the case to next-door Warrick County for trial after a grand jury indicted all three for murder and robbery. Paul Wever (the prosecuting attorney in Ziemer's 1952 morals case) represented William Thompson and argued that his campaign for Vanderburgh County prosecutor would take up too much time for a summer trial. The new judge, Addison Beavers, set a new trial date of November 9, 1964, the day after the election. Prosecutor Roberts announced that he would be seeking the death penalty for all three, whom the judge ruled would be tried together rather than separately.[43] This unwittingly set in motion a series of events that would change the outcome and the value of LGBTQ lives for nearly twenty years.

For several days, the 3 clean-cut, neatly dressed defendants sat quietly listening to the questions asked of nearly 140 prospective jurors. Most were dismissed by the prosecution when they expressed their opposition to the death penalty. Witnesses observed that women looked more at the 3 young men sitting across from the jury box than at the questioner.

In the case of male jurors, many of whom approved of the death penalty in the case of murder, the questions were different.[44]

Howard Sandusky, who had successfully defended James Duncan Holcombe in 1961 in the Burdette murder case, asked each male juror these questions:

"Have you ever been approached by a homosexual?"

"Do you believe a man has the right to defend himself against homosexual advances?"

"Are you familiar with Rudolph Ziemer's reputation as a homosexual?"

In some cases, the prosecution would excuse a juror for one of their answers; in some cases, the defense would excuse. But at the end of the third day, an all-male jury of white, middle-aged to older men was seated. The trial began on Monday, November 16, 1964, with prosecution witnesses starting with sheriff's deputy Lee West, who pulled Ziemer's body out of the Dodge station wagon after the car was pulled from the brown water of the Ohio River that chilly March afternoon.

"Was the body that of the man who was charged with sodomy three times in the last seventeen years?" asked Sandusky, beginning his attack on the dead victim. Prosecutor Roberts objected, saying Ziemer was not on trial, and the judge agreed, telling the jury to disregard that question.

Roberts told the jury of the events of the evening of March 12, 1963—that the men beat Ziemer and robbed him, leaving him in his car near the Colonial Manor apartments, but they came back, fearing their fingerprints were on the car and that Ziemer, if awakened, could identify them. Roberts stated that they returned to the car and took it and Ziemer to the levee on Weinbach Avenue, pushing it into the water so that he would drown, thus showing premeditation.

For several days, witnesses came and went, presenting what ordinarily would be a tight case for murder. The deputy coroner, Dr. Donald Godwin, testified through myriad scenarios by the three defense attorneys that despite Ziemer's blood alcohol level (0.28 at the time of the autopsy on March 14), the cause of death had to be drowning, not choking on his own vomit or any other cause.

The prosecution called witness after witness stating the obvious: Ziemer had been beaten, robbed and his unconscious body left in the flooded Ohio River to die by these three clean-cut, all-American GIs whose service in the military had ended while awaiting trial. Pirrie had married Melvina Shutt in the months prior to the trial. All three sets of parents were in the courtroom, as was Pirrie's new three-month-old son periodically. Sandusky smartly sat Melvina and the baby in the front where the all-male jury could easily see them.

During the trial proceedings on November 18, arguments erupted between the defense attorneys when the signed confession of William Thompson was entered into evidence. Pirrie and Graymont had declined to make statements at the arrest and were not in the room with Thompson when he signed his statement showing they had pushed the car into the river with Ziemer still alive. Lopp, attorney for Pirrie, demanded his client be tried separately from the other two. Sandusky, attorney for Graymont, did the same.[45]

Judge Beavers ruled he felt he could adequately instruct the jurors in this matter and overruled the move to split the trial up into three parts. This was another in a significant series of events that almost certainly affected the verdict in this case.

November 19 saw the courtroom erupt into a cacophony of charges and countercharges.[46]

Wever questioned Evansville police sergeant Donald Gooch, who had interviewed Thompson and taken his statement on March 14. Gooch testified Thompson told him he had pushed the car into about four feet of water and opened the door and stepped out, leaving the still-breathing Ziemer. Gooch went on to say Thompson told him Ziemer had been "pawing him" in the car, offering to buy him a bottle of whiskey if he would come back to his house with him. Thompson said that was when he started beating Ziemer, and Pirrie joined in while they were near the Colonial Manor apartments.

Carol Sue Gentry, the other young woman with the group that evening, was called to the witness stand near the end of the day and related a story that had occurred the week before. She was at home when there was a knock on her door. When she opened it, there stood Melvina and Patrick Pirrie, who asked to come in and talk to her. She let them in.

Pirrie told her that she needed to refuse to testify in the case because if she didn't testify "there is no case, don't you see. You're the only witness."

Gentry said Melvina warned her that if she testified, she would be charged as an accessory to murder if the men were convicted because she had driven them all around that night, and she would go to prison too. Gentry was scared. Melvina had been her friend for a long time, and she didn't want to be in trouble. She called the prosecutor, Roberts, who advised her that she was not under threat of arrest, although she was a material witness and as such could not leave the city. She also related that during the evening, she and Thompson had discussed dating, but at the end of the night, Thompson told her given what all had occurred, it would be best if they didn't. Melvina said that Gentry held all the cards because she and Pirrie were married now and she could not be compelled to testify against her husband.

Melvina was called to the witness stand and asked about this instance of witness tampering. She said she had gotten the idea that she and Carol could be charged as accessories by Roberts himself while they were being held in custody immediately after the body was found and the GIs returned from Fort Campbell. "You know that's not true, Melvina," retorted Roberts.[47]

The Verdict

The final day of the trial of the three ex-GIs, November 23, was cold and windy outside the historic courthouse in Boonville, Indiana. The three defense attorneys for Patrick Pirrie, Robert Graymont and William Thompson did not call a single witness. Instead, all three immediately moved to their summations to the jury and in blistering terms put the dead Rudolph Ziemer on trial, much the same way the British Queens Bench had done with Oscar Wilde seventy-odd years earlier.[48]

Throughout the trial, defense attorneys peppered witnesses with questions concerning the reputation of Ziemer. The police officers and detectives were all asked if they were aware of Ziemer's past history of arrests for sodomy and if they had heard he was a "sexual pervert." This particular word had a deep meaning in the ears of the all-male Warrick County jury, as an eleven-year-old girl had recently been assaulted and murdered in the county, and headlines had screamed that word repeatedly.

Lopp told the jury, "I have no doubt my client hit him. He should have hit him. This case should only be a charge of assault and battery, not murder. They had the right to defend themselves against an old drunken pervert."

Sandusky, attorney for Graymont, blamed Roberts for causing the whole situation because he hadn't rounded up all the "old sexual perverts long ago. I'm not going to be as nice as Mr. Lopp. To me a queer is just a queer, plain and simple. Mr. Graymont is not guilty of anything other than driving around in a car with Carol Gentry, if anyone should be indicted here; it should be her."

It was in the ensuing moments when evidence was presented from a tip that one of the jurors, a man named Wathen, had been seen in the Old Kentucky Barbeque (the place Ziemer made his fatal stop) the night before with William Thompson and Kay Goble, the girl to whose apartment the group had adjourned that dreadful night in March. The juror was

THE EVANSVILLE COURIER

Final Home Edition

THE WEATHER—Warmer... Page 8

9TH YEAR—NO. 277 | EVANSVILLE, IND., TUESDAY MORNING, NOVEMBER 24, 1964 | 26 PAGES | TEN CENTS

Three Ex-Paratroopers Cleared In Ziemer Death

Jury Stays Out Hour and Half; Juror Charged

By SUZANNE PORTER
Courier Staff Writer

BOONVILLE, Ind.—Three young men accused of murdering Rudolph Ziemer were freed by a Warrick County Circuit Court jury here Monday night.

It took the all-male jury 1½ hours to decide that ex-paratroopers William Thompson, 22, of East Gary, Ind.; Patrick Pirrie, 21, of Southgate, Calif., and Robert Greymont, 25, of Needham, Mass., were not guilty of murder in the death of the 56-year-old funeral director.

One of the jurors said later most of that time was spent deliberating over Thompson. The jury was in agreement on the first ballot that neither Greymont nor Pirrie was guilty, he said.

Juror Dismissed

The jury began deliberating about 7 p.m. after a day that had included the dismissal of one juror for contempt of court and resting of the case by the defense without a single witness. There was also a motion by the prosecution to revoke the bail of all three defendants.

With the finding of "not guilty," the latter motion became immaterial.

Juror James J. Wathen, a Warrick County farmer and Alcoa employe, was ordered to appear Dec. 11 to answer charges of contempt of court.

Vanderburgh County Prosecutor O. H. Roberts Jr. was seeking the death penalty for all three men.

Death Penalty Sought

They were charged with murdering Ziemer by driving his car into the backwaters of the Ohio River and leaving him there on March 12, 1963. The body was dragged from the river March 14, 1963.

The state alleged that Ziemer had been beaten and robbed before he was left to die in the water.

Attorneys for both the state and the defense presented closing arguments during the afternoon.

Defense attorneys lashed out unmercifully throughout the afternoon at the reputation of Ziemer, constantly referring to him as a "pervert."

Policemen Testify

Under cross-examination, two Evansville police officers had testified last week that Ziemer was well known in Evansville as a sexual pervert.

James Lopp, attorney for Pirrie, told the jury that the case should be no more than an assault and battery case.

"He (Pirrie) hit him," Lopp said. "There's no doubt in my mind he hit him. They had a right to defend themselves from a drunken pervert."

Lopp and Howard Sandusky, Greymont's attorney, both accused Prosecutor Roberts of withholding evidence and criticized him for not "rounding up all the old perverts" in Evansville. They charged that the ball point pen taken from Ziemer's clothing, his wallet, wristwatch, and eyeglasses should have been presented as evidence.

Defense Claims Noted

All three defense attorneys claimed the prosecution had not proved the cause of death, the allegations contained in the indictment, nor premeditation.

Paul Wever, attorney for Thompson, who admitted to Evansville detectives that he had driven the car into the water, told the jury the prosecution had presented no evidence that the three men knew the car would move further into the water until it was completely submerged, as alleged in the indictment.

"The only thing poor Bob Greymont is guilty of is taking a ride in a car driven by Carol Gentry, who should have been indicted if anyone was indicted because she drove the car that led them around," Sandusky told the jury.

Outlines Testimony

Terry Dietsch, assistant prosecuting attorney, outlined testimony of prosecution witnesses for the jury. Warrick County Prosecutor Burley Scales and Vanderburgh County Prosecutor Roberts summed up final arguments for the prosecution.

"We're not on trial here," Scales told the jury, referring to comments regarding himself and Roberts. "Neither am I going to defend Rudolph Ziemer. He is dead by the acts of these three men."

Scales repeated testimony of Dr. Donald Godwin, pathologist who performed the autopsy, that Ziemer had died of asphyxiation by drowning.

Roberts said he believed evidence showed the three men

(Continued on Page 2, Column 8)

Win Fight for Life: These three former paratroopers were acquitted by a jury Monday night of murder in connection with the death of Rudolph Ziemer. Shown outside the courtroom in Boonville Monday are William Thompson (left), Robert Greymont (center), and Patrick Pirrie.

Courier Photo by Sonny Brown

Verdict Lifts Shadow From Three Lives; Strain Gives Way to Tears

U.S.-Airlifted Troops Rescue Congo Hostages

WASHINGTON (Tuesday) (AP) — Belgian paratroopers, carried by U.S. transport planes, moved into rebel-held Stanleyville in The Congo at dawn Tuesday and the State Department said that about three hours later foreign hostages were pouring into the airport.

Plane Noses Over, Kills 44 In Italy

Estes Put In Jail, Released

Interest Rate To Banks Goes Up

Planes Ram; Three Killed

In Today's Courier

Above: *Evansville Courier*, November 24, 1964. The killers of Rudolph Ziemer are acquitted of murder in a scandalous trial. *Evansville Vanderburgh Public Library*.

Opposite: *Evansville Press*, November 24, 1964. Ziemer killers and families after the jury acquits them of murder. The defense put Ziemer on trial. *Evansville Vanderburgh Public Library*.

The "not guilty" verdict in the Rudolph Ziemer case was cause for celebration among the three defendants and close relatives last night in the Warrick County courthouse. From left, the group included Mrs. William Thompson, mother of William Thompson, one of the defendants who stood next to her; Mrs. Melvin Shutt, mother-in-law of another defendant, Patrick Pirrie, who stood next to her; Pirrie's wife, Melvina, who is holding the couple's three-month-old son, Danny; Pirrie's brother, Bob; Mrs. Sally Greymont, wife of the third defendant, Robert Greymont, who is next to her. The woman on the extreme right is Mrs. Walter Greymont, mother of the defendant. (Staff Photo by Bill Lamneck)

Not Guilty Verdict in Ziemer Case Climaxes Emotion-Packed Day

By ROBERT FLYNN
Press Staff Writer

BOONVILLE—The not guilty verdicts in the Rudolph Ziemer murder case came last night shortly after 8:30—the peak of an emotion-packed day in the 60-year-old Warrick County courthouse.

the three Evansville defense attorneys. Howard Sandusky, James Lopp and Paul Wever.

Even the 50 or so spectators who were there out of curiosity seemed pleased with the verdict.

An older juror who had already filed past the defendants stopped to watch the scene which only a

gear shift was in "drive" and the emergency brake was off.

WEVER'S speech concentrated on the prosecution's duty to prove "beyond a reasonable doubt" that the death was caused by someone who left the Ziemer car "well-knowing that it would

2 Children Die In Explosion

KANSAS CITY, Mo. — (UPI) — Firemen today recovered the bodies of two children killed in an explosion that ripped apart a three-story apartment building near downtown Kansas City.

The victims were Debra Brown,

dismissed and warned of a possible contempt charge. Amazingly, Goble and Thompson were not called on to answer for their actions, although the prosecution did ask that bond be revoked, which was overruled.[49] Roberts, in his summation, made the following statement: "Homosexuality is not a crime; it is an unfortunate condition. They killed Rudolph Ziemer because they didn't like homosexuals. Next time they may kill because they don't like Negroes or Jews or gray-haired people. The three defendants want you to accept their right to play God because that's exactly what they did the night they killed Rudolph Ziemer."[50]

It took the jury one hour and thirty minutes to reach a verdict: all three were judged not guilty. The jury foreman related that most of the deliberation was about Thompson because of his confession, but they felt since the three were tried together, they should have the same verdict. The three defendants shook hands with each juror. One older juror admonished Thompson's parents to "make sure he goes to church."

And it was done. The next morning, the newspapers had a photograph of the smiling defendants, their families and the Pirries' new baby on the front page. For a decade, schoolboys would hurl the epithet "you're a Rudy Ziemer" at any other boy who was perceived as a sissy on Evansville school playgrounds. The murdered funeral home owner's memory lived on as a pejorative for a short time and then faded as time passed and people forgot about the killing and its injustice.

CHAPTER 6

EVANSVILLE GOES TO THE MOVIES

Evansville has had a love affair with movies since the earliest silent nickelodeons opened in the early 1900s. In the days before television, the city had many movie theaters that switched to sound as soon as the technology was available in the late 1920s. The quality of the theaters ranged from the elegant New Grand and Victory movie palaces, which also had live performances and large seating capacities, to small neighborhood movie houses with smaller screens and more limited space. First-run films were normally shown at the major downtown theaters first, later moving to smaller houses as newer studio releases came to town.

LGBTQ characters and themes were officially outlawed by the 1934 Breen Production Code, which specifically forbade, among other things, "sex perversion." Even though a perceptive audience member could identify certain characteristics in actors like Franklin Pangborn or Eric Blore or characters like male dress designers with effeminate mannerisms, it wasn't until the late production code era, when European films with much looser moral themes began stealing American movie audiences, that the Breen code began to crumble.

Evansville, being a major motion picture release market by the 1950s, was shocked at the 1959 film *Suddenly, Last Summer*, made from the Tennessee Williams play and starring Elizabeth Taylor, Montgomery Clift (gay in his personal life) and Katharine Hepburn. Audiences knew the theme of the play was of an adult nature. Karl Knecht, the *Evansville Courier*'s daily cartoonist and writer of an arts column, saw the first release of the film on a trip to New York before it came to town. He reported the themes of the film were disturbing and dealt with "homosexualism" and "cannibalism," but he thought, according to the paper's movie reviewer Jeanne Suhrheinrich, that Evansville audiences might not realize those are the themes in seeing the film.

Suhrheinrich warned audiences in an April 1, 1960 review that the film was absolutely only for an adult audience that could handle serious and sometimes nauseating themes. The movie traced the last European vacation of a wealthy young New Orleans man, accompanied by his troubled but lovely cousin (Liz), who herself was recovering from a rape (another theme rarely dealt with). During the vacation, he molests and then humiliates a whole herd of young men in a remote Spanish coastal city. At one hideous moment, he pays for his sin of homosexuality by being murdered and devoured by his "victims" atop a Roman ruin.

The whole thing has led the cousin to near madness, and the gay man's mother (Hepburn) wants the surgeon (Clift) to perform a lobotomy to remove any possible memory that would taint her son's reputation. Through hypnosis, the cousin is forced to remember what she witnessed, and the mother then lapses into madness herself.

Suhrheinrich said that Williams had made a name for himself by exploring the most hideous and odious parts of the human psyche and that this film might be disturbing to viewers. Bish Thompson, reviewer for the *Press*, had about the same reaction.[51]

The next film that came to Evansville and caused a sensation with a homosexual theme (and drew some concerned locals to write to the newspaper about controlling films coming to town with a censorship board) was *The Children's Hour*. Lillian Helman had written the story many years earlier, and a watered-down version of the story was filmed in the stricter 1930s, leaving out its lesbian theme, but in the 1961 version, it was front and center. Audrey Hepburn and Shirley MacLaine play two young women who are lifelong friends and open a boarding school in New England for privileged girls.

A student who is being punished for bullying her peers tells her grandmother (Fay Bainter) a lie that she has seen the two women engaged in lesbian sex. The grandmother pulls the girl out of school and tells the other families this lie. The school is near collapse, and the women file a slander suit against the grandmother. It is during the terrible trial that Shirley MacLaine's character realizes (out of nowhere) that indeed she is a lesbian and has caused this whole disaster by her unconscious love for

Hepburn's character. The story ends with MacLaine hanging herself and Hepburn finding her after her confession. The film goes a little further to assure audiences that while the one lesbian is safely dead, the object of her affection is going to go on and have a nice heterosexual relationship with a local physician played by James Garner.

The Children's Hour drew a much more sympathetic review from Suhrheinrich, with her review stressing the sadness of the story and the value of the film's sticking to Hellman's actual play. Again, she warned audiences that the film was strictly for adults. Remember, this was long before any movie rating system was in place, and local audiences relied on theater owners and reviewers to guide them.[52]

Advise and Consent

Allen Drury's first big dramatic political novel, *Advise and Consent*, was published in 1959 and follows the controversial nomination of a liberal as the nation's secretary of state by an unpopular president. Leading the fight against the nomination is a charismatic young senator from Utah, Brig Anderson, who is exposed by pro-communist sympathizers to have had a homosexual liaison during the war with another soldier who has sold love letters and pictures of the two to Anderson's enemies. When the exposure happens, Anderson commits suicide.

The novel was a bestseller and became a Broadway play. The Evansville Broadway Theater League was a popular group of the city's elite who raised funds to bring touring companies to Evansville and perform current plays at the Victory Theater. *Advise and Consent*, the play, came to Evansville in October 1961 starring Farley Granger, a Hollywood actor who was gay in his personal life. The league made sure to advertise the play as being for adults only.[53]

In July 1962, the film version premiered at the New Grand Theater (its final presentation before it was demolished) and won high praise from Suhrheinrich, who encouraged adults only to flock to see it. Brig Anderson's character in the film version is played by Don Murray. In the film, unlike the play, America and Evansville, in one unforgettable scene, have a peek into what gay bars were like in 1961: dark, underground, mysterious places where effeminate men pawed each other as Frank Sinatra records played in the background. Murray's character has traced his former male lover to this bar, and when he sees him again, enraged that this man has blackmailed him and repulsed by the bar patrons, he shoves the man into the gutter as his taxi flees the scene.[54]

One other film from the early 1960s that played in Evansville for exactly one week was a Dirk Bogarde vehicle from England. The film *Victim* deals with the then-current problem of homosexual men in England being blackmailed. Great Britain didn't end its anti-gay laws that had ensnared Oscar Wilde until 1968. *Victim* did not play at the major theaters downtown, being screened only at the East Side Washington Theater, a neighborhood movie house. The fact that it played in Evansville at all seems a miracle today. No evidence exists as to its audience numbers, and neither daily paper reviewed it.

Several letter writers bemoaned this new "homosexual" angle that movies from Hollywood were taking, and some longed for the good old days when "everyone could see every movie" and none were strictly for adults. As the 1960s progressed, films began expressing homosexual themes more often, but always at the end, the gay persons paid for their sins with death, either by suicide or by a convenient lightning strike to a tree, as happened to Sandy Dennis's lesbian character in *The Fox* in 1967. In movies, a woman committing adultery might be put out in the storm (*Stella Dallas*, 1937), but if she is a lesbian, she just has to die.

By 1970, Evansville audiences had gotten used to the dead homosexual (1968's *The Detective*, with Sinatra as a detective investigating a gay murder, has two dead homosexuals). So it was a little bit of a shock when Mart Crowley's surprise hit 1968 play *The Boys in the Band* came to the screen in the River City at the Loew's Majestic, the poor cousin of the Loew's Victory Theater and located in a different part of downtown, during the Fourth of July weekend.

Crowley's story has an all-male cast in a dramatic tale of an ill-fated birthday party. All of the men except one are homosexual. Crowley wrote the story from experiences in his own life to show the pain and psychological trauma gay men experienced over the course of their lives in America at that time.

In her review, Suhrheinrich still warned readers the film dealt with homosexuality but said this:

> *If you can accept that a film about homosexuality can be hilariously funny to begin with, and movingly sad to end with, you'll find the movie excellent both from a technical and entertainment viewpoint. It has words not used in polite conversation so be warned. The cast is flawless in its portrayal of Crowley's original work which is, despite its black acidic and funny dialogue, a serious social work.*[55]

Courier Photo by Sonny Brown

Birthday boys: **Bob Harris, as birthday honoree, Tom Angermeier as party host, and Tim McDaniel as surprise gift, are key members of "The Boys in the Band," now at the ISUE Playhouse under the direction of Jim Jackson.**

Publicity photo for ISUE production of *Boys in the Band*, 1974. *Evansville Vanderburgh Public Library*.

In the *Evansville Press*, reviewer Bill Gumberts called it "top entertainment."[56]

Suhrheinrich got a second chance to review the work, as the late Jim Jackson, theater director at the then–Indiana State University of Evansville, produced *Boys in the Band* at the college's theater in July 1974. She wrote that the story wouldn't "create any shock waves in the community as it might have just a few short years ago. A hit in 1968 precisely because of that shock value, in 1974 it will be judged on its own dramatic values." Suhrheinrich said in her opinion the story had achieved mainstream acceptance because a short revival in New England had caused demonstrations by "gay libbers" who bemoaned the work as a detriment to their cause by presenting homosexual men as neurotic drunks tormenting one another.[57]

The Supreme Court's ruling striking down most national obscenity laws in the early 1970s led to an explosion nationwide in the pornography industry. Once the bastion of cheap 8mm home movies men kept hidden in their garages or magazines under their mattresses, pornography boomed into an open environment of access to such materials. In the 1960s, there were several raids on local newsstands that sold adult-type magazines behind the counter. In one case, a customer asked for a certain magazine, decided he didn't want it and put it on a regular rack, where it was seen by an underage boy. Police arrested the salesclerk, and the business paid a stiff fine.

By the mid-1970s, there were no fewer than four adult shops in Evansville selling books, magazines and home movies (later VHS cassettes). An adult bookstore on SE Third Street in the business district was quickly shut down.

On the West Side, the former Franklin Theater, a neighborhood movie house that for years showed family films such as westerns, was purchased by a new owner and converted into the infamous Studio Art Theater. The Studio Art became a draw for both homosexual and heterosexual audiences and the "curious" who explored their sexuality in the confines of the adult theater and its adjoining store. The Studio Art was well known in the entire tristate area and drew religious protesters periodically, who picketed outside and across the street. Eventually, the city and county government passed zoning restrictions that all but eliminated new such businesses in

entertainment The Evansville Courier
Saturday, February 20, 1982

'Making Love' is a love story with a twist

By PATRICE SMITH
Courier staff writer

Review

Though it reputedly "arrived" in Hollywood during the late Sixties, homosexuality generally has been avoided by major film producers as an fit subject for the western cinema — too risky or too risque, they thought.

When the topic was addressed — which was quite often, actually — references to homosexuality were made in terms of intimation ("The Maltese Falcon"), criminal behavior ("Advise and Consent," "The Best Man"), humor (in "That Touch of Mink," Gig Young's psychiatrist thought he was in love with Cary Grant) or social statement ("Midnight Cowboy.").

Despite Arthur Miller's "A View from the Bridge" with its first male kiss, the TV-movie "That Certain Summer" and France's "Le Cage I and II" with the breezy acceptance of unorthodox lifestyles, American filmgoers seem reluctant to accept a straight-forward treatment of sexual preference.

The marketeers of Twentieth Century-Fox knew they faced a tough sell with "Making Love," reportedly significant because it represents the first time a major studio has made a film dealing sympathetically with homosexuality. So Fox is employing some fanciful sales strategies to sell "Making Love" to the public in three different ways:

To gays, "Making Love" is presented as it is, a sympathetic view of a homosexual's "coming out." To the mainstream audience, it is being sold as a "women's film" — Hollywoodese for a "soap opera." To young, educated men, it is peddled as an "important film event" — a "serious film" which serious filmgoers should see.

Did big screen salesfolks assume "Making Love" would not stand on its own merit as an entertaining, decent, intelligently conceived and well executed movie about human relationships, homosexuality or no? Evidently they did, and that's a shame because "Making Love" is not the big deal Fox thinks it is.

Undoubtedly, some fuss will be made over "Making Love," particularly in more conservative areas such as the Midwest. But until moviegoers see the film, or discuss it with someone who has, protesters' presumptions are meaningless.

"Making Love" is not a great film, but it is a candid and literate treatment of a contemporary issue which exists in the boardrooms and executive suites as well as 42nd Street and Haight Ashbury. Even more, it is a story about understanding, about compassion for those who may be different from ourselves.

"Making Love" focuses on a happy marriage — a rarity anyway — which is destroyed by an intruder, not a third party, really, but an increasing doubt and eventual confirmation about one partner's sexuality. While such a tale could be maudlin, soapy and redundant, "Making Love" is refreshingly real and wryly witty — an undeniable entertainment.

Kate Jackson demonstrates depth of emotion she never had a chance to show as "The Rookies" angel of mercy or the posturing Sabrina of "Charlie's Angels." Director Arthur Hiller ("The Americanization of Emily," "Love Story" and "Silver Streak," among many others) wisely chooses to focus equal attention on Ms. Jackson's Claire, a bright, up-and-coming TV executive, and on Claire's physician husband Zack.

At the film's start, Hiller and screenwriter Barry Sandler effectively establish the fully satisfying, stimulating relationship enjoyed by Claire and Zack. They recite old movie dialogue to their Betamax, sing old Gilbert and Sullivan operettas to each other, dine weekly with poetry-spouting neighbor Dame Wendy Hiller, agree to pinch pennies so they can buy a lavish Hollywood Hills dream home and tentatively talk about a baby.

In a brief, significant scene, they attend a rowdy country bar's amateur show and witness a dowdy little Lucie Lee (Erica Hiller) almost capture the contest booby prize for her sorry tune. Before she is booed off the stage, Zack and Claire jump to their feet, volunteer to compete and proceed to perform a hilarious, improvised country version of Gilbert and Sullivan. When the announcer exclaims, "It looks like little Lucie Lee won't be gettin' the booby prize after all," the appreciation and relief glowing from her face make their point — "Making Love" is not just about gays after all.

Michael Ontkean's Zack, though happy with his family-oriented doctoring and his feisty, attractive wife, notices a strange, frightening absence in his life. Then he meets Bart (Harry Hamlin), a brilliant, successful young fiction writer who arrives at the doctor's office for apparent hypochondria and soon becomes a good friend. On impulse, the troubled physician contacts the free (and, it turns out, quite easy) writer for a dinner engagement. They become lovers.

But scripter Barry Sandler adds an insightful twist into the already uncomfortable situation: Hamlin's Bart, unlike Ontkean's sensitive, kind Zack, is a vain, smug, self-involved creep. While Zack yearns for his newly discovered life of loving, Bart stubbornly cruises gay bars, defending his "right" to a life of one-night-stands.

The interplay of emotions and conflicts is frankly addressed throughout "Making Love." And the love scene (count 'em — one) is tasteful and shot with deliberate caution, as if Hiller were saying to his mainstream audience, "I'll break this to you very gently."

Performances by the three principals are nothing short of outstanding: Ms. Jackson's range is broad, her inner turmoil subtly and effectively conveyed. Ontkean communicates Zack as a caring, idealistic and fully masculine man, a delightfully unique characterization for a doctor. Hamlin is deliciously schizophrenic as the bitchy bar cruiser who writes from an imprisoned heart.

"Making Love" sacrifices cinematic artistry for its story, but James Vance's lensing makes room for fine lighting effects, symbolic splits into threes and dark, oily street scenes. Occasionally, the film's flow is broken by close-up, white-backed reminiscences of Claire and Bart talking to somebody — possibly the audience. The first-person accounts interrupt the action to no worthwhile effect.

Rated R for its adult theme, "Making Love" is a clean, honest tearjerker. It continues this weekend at East Park Cinemas.

MICHAEL ONTKEAN

Evansville Courier, March 1982, review of *Making Love*. *Evansville Vanderburgh Public Library*.

most areas of town. The management of the Studio Art eventually made a fatal error by offering live nude performances by women in one part of the business, which led to its closing after a ten-year legal battle in 1997. The case reached all the way to the U.S. Supreme Court, which in the end declined to hear the case, leading to the theater's eventual closure. The building was demolished in 2001.

For Evansville moviegoers, 1982 was the year homosexual relationships burst upon them in a series of films that played in suburban cinemas. The downtown movie houses had passed into oblivion by that time, and theaters were multiple-screened complexes where the great melting pot of local movie audiences met.

In the early spring, the film *Making Love*, starring Kate Jackson, Michael Ontkean and Harry Hamlin, opened at East Park Cinema 5 and drew large audiences who sometimes acted out during the scene where Ontkean and Hamlin kiss. Several residents wrote letters to the editors of the daily papers about it, but in this case, they were writing to complain about the audience members who were loudly hooting the movie, not about the subject matter.

Other films that came to Evansville that year included *Personal Best*, a love story about lesbian athletes that prompted a very touching review by *Evansville Press* critic Nancy Wick, who wrote, "1982 seems to be the year homosexual relationships have come out of the movie theater closet. From the straight drama *Making Love* to the spoof *Partners* to the mystery *Deathtrap*, movie audiences have been exposed to gay relationships right and left." Such a description of Hollywood offerings would have only been dreamed of just ten years earlier in Evansville. Another film that opened here in March 1982 was *Victor, Victoria*, about a down-on-her-luck singer (Julie Andrews) who begins to impersonate a man, impersonating a woman, in a French drag revue. The film drew very positive reviews (possibly because underneath the ruse, the main characters were heterosexual), but the gay themes throughout the film and a surprise ending with a relationship between two of the male characters as a twist didn't even register on our Evansville movie Richter scale. We had indeed come a long way.

CHAPTER 7

KENNETH SANDERS

1966

The Apartment

At the southeast corner of First Street and Chandler Avenue in the heart of Evansville, Indiana's Preservation District, an area primarily made up of ornate mid- to late Victorian mansions built by the city's barons in the nineteenth century before such things as income tax or expensive utility costs, there sits a squat, two-story unadorned apartment house. Winged by an exterior stairway that provides access to the two flats on the second floor, the building, constructed during the World War II housing shortage, is a stark contrast to its neighbors.

The building contains four very small apartments, each with two rooms and kitchen with bath. Rents at the building were always low, and many times, the tenants living there disturbed the more genteel neighbors in the surrounding grander homes. Loud music, loud parties and general mayhem followed some of the tenants through the years.

One tenant, Kenneth Sanders, who lived in 703B, upper left, was never any trouble. A graduate of Benjamin Bosse High School in the class of 1957, Sanders had worked as an antique dealer and auctioneer for Ray Minton at the Auction Barn, located on the North Side, for six years. He bought the business outright in 1963 and took over as house auctioneer. Sanders was a community volunteer in the early 1960s, dressing in a Santa costume to help charities deliver presents to needy children and hosting political auctions when the local Democrats called on him.

In order to earn more money, in early 1966, when he turned twenty-seven, he applied for and secured an assembly-line job at the local Whirlpool plant, which made refrigerators. He worked many hours a week and conducted auctions when he was hired. Sanders had quite a few well-connected friends in the community, although most never visited him at his small apartment after he moved out of his parents' house on East Indiana Street.

Flat Iron

Tall and lanky, dressed in his uniform from the gas station where he worked, nineteen-year-old Larry Eugene Williams sat in his pickup truck in the parking lot of the Wesselman's supermarket on Claremont Avenue on the West Side of Evansville in the very early morning hours of March 15, 1966, nearly three years to the day after Rudolph Ziemer's car was found in the Ohio River. It was nippy outside, but he waited nervously for an Evansville police officer he knew to meet him there. It was about 3:30 a.m. and very quiet where he waited. Earlier, he had flagged down a police cruiser and asked the two officers in the car if they knew whether Ted Karges was working the night shift. They radioed in and found out he was. It was an unusual request, but Williams asked if Karges, the only officer he personally knew, could meet him here. Karges radioed that he would and that Williams should wait.

Karges drove up beside Williams, who asked if he could accompany him back to a friend's apartment to check things out. Williams suspected something was very wrong and was afraid to go alone. Karges followed him to the apartment building on SE First Street. Williams told Karges that at about 3:00 a.m., he had pulled up in front of the building and climbed the stairs on the side, intending to knock on Kenneth Sanders's door. He said he needed some cash and Sanders had always helped him out.

Williams said just as he set foot on the second-floor balcony, another man about Sanders's age came out of Sanders's apartment. Williams asked him if Ken was awake. The man said Sanders wasn't home, but he knew where he was if Williams would drive him there. The man was drunk, but it wasn't unusual for young drunken men to come in and out of Sanders's apartment at that hour, so Williams said yes. He said he immediately regretted agreeing to drive him anywhere because he noticed that Sanders's car was parked on the street across from the apartment building. Why would his car be there if he were not?

The man told Williams to drive to Sanders's business, the Auction Barn on Heidelbach Avenue, because that's where he was. It took about ten minutes to get there, but the building was dark and locked. No sign of Sanders. The man got back in the truck and asked a final favor. Would Williams drop him at Ruby's Diner, a little breakfast house on North Main Street that was open at that hour? Williams agreed only because he was certain someone would be at Ruby's and he could get away from this man. On the drive to the diner, Williams noticed his passenger was wiping his hands on a handkerchief that was bloodied.

"Been in a fight?" he asked. The man replied, "Yeah." He said he'd had to hit some "faggot" over the head with something metal and had gotten blood on himself. Pulling up in front of Ruby's, Williams said the man dropped the cloth on the floor of the truck and got out. Williams drove off as quickly as he could. This was why he had called Karges and wanted him to accompany him to Sanders's apartment.

Together, they climbed the staircase and walked to the second floor. The door was open, and the apartment was dark. When Karges flipped on the light, the main room was littered with beer cans and ashtrays. It appeared there had been several people in the small apartment by the number of empty cans and heavy smell of smoke. The bedroom was just beyond the small kitchen.

On the floor next to the rumpled bed was the body of a man lying on his back and wearing only a pair of jockey shorts. His body was bloody, and Karges saw that his face had been beaten in, his eye sockets crushed. His head was turned so that Karges could see the back of his skull was also crushed. They assumed it was Sanders because his eyeglasses were lying beside him, and Williams recognized them. The bedroom and living room had been ransacked, drawers pulled out and papers scattered everywhere. Karges telephoned the police station and asked for Detective Jess Julian to meet them.

There were numerous fingerprints on the beer cans and ashtrays. Julian estimated there had been at least three or four people in the apartment. There was an antique flatiron, the type that a housewife in pre-electric days would heat on a stove until hot and iron clothes with, covered in blood. Someone had put a pillow under Sanders's battered head; it, too, was bloody. It appeared someone had tried to clean himself up in the bathroom. Blood had been trailed in there and was in the sink and bathtub.

Williams was taken to jail and held as an accessory after the fact for murder along with another young man who was never identified but who was soon

The Evansville Press

FINAL HOME EDITION

60TH YEAR—NO. 220 | EVANSVILLE, IND., TUESDAY, MARCH 15, 1966 | 20 PAGES | PRICE TEN CENTS

EC To Be University Of Evansville

By EDNA FOLZ

Evansville College trustees today approved changing the name of the school to the University of Evansville.

The trustees also approved a boost in tuition rates beginning next September; they designated 15 new faculty positions for the 1966-67 school year, and approved a $4,239,000 operating budget.

In authorizing the name change to the University of Evansville, the trustees also decided to present a bill to the 1967 Indiana Legislature to amend the school's charter to coincide with today's step.

Another story and picture on Page 9.

DR. MELVIN HYDE, college president, said: "On several occasions in recent years I have referred to a future plan for changing the name of Evansville College to the University of Evansville.

"The major difference between a college and a university involves size as well as the number of administrative educational units. Last fall the college enrolled about 2800 full-time and 2200 part-time students. We have a school of engineering, a school of nursing, a community college, and an accredited master's degree program for teachers.

"Other areas where there are possibilities for administrative changes include liberal arts, business administration and economics, fine arts, and education."

The 1966-67 operating budget is the first in the school's history to exceed $4 million and is $800,000 more than the 1965-66 operating budget. The figure does not include capital outlay for new construction.

The tuition rate increase will be $20 per quarter. This, plus a raise from $12.50 to $13 per quarter in student activity fees, means a total for tuition and fees for a full-time student of $864 for a three-quarter academic year.

Also beginning in September the new rate for the community college will be $16 per quarter credit hour — an increase of $1.

IN A LETTER mailed to EC students and parents today, Ralph Olmsted, college treasurer and business manager, pointed out that a survey of 13 colleges in Indiana comparable to Evansville showed 11 of them are raising tuition. Of the 13 colleges, Evansville will still have the lowest tuition rate — 31 per cent below the average of the 13, Olmsted said.

He cited the need for "excellent instruction" and the "steadily rising quality of teaching at Evansville College."

The increased operating budget will provide for the 15 new faculty positions, plus a merit increase for faculty and staff.

Hyde, while not discussing faculty pay, has said that during past years EC has been giving annual merit pay increases.

INSIDE THE PRESS

GOP Chiefs Offer Foreign Aid Plan

HOUSE Republican leaders, in another "minority" position, suggest ways of improving the 20-year-old foreign aid program, Page 2.

PARLIAMENT stormed into its fourth day of noisy, name-calling debate today concerning the alleged sex scandal that jeopardized the security of Canada. Page 3.

THE ONE and only Andres Segovia, world's best guitarist, is one of the artists signed up by the Musicians' Club for its 1966-67 concert series. Page 5.

A 'Happy Hour,' On the House

OXFORD, N. J. — (UPI) — Free cocktails before dinner at county welfare homes?

A regular cocktail time or "happy hour" could save a welfare house more than $2000 a year on tranquilizers, according to Mrs. Mildred Ochse, Warren County Wel-

U.S. Copter Rescues Six Under Fire

Enemy Mortar Fire Sinks Heavy Plane Off Viet Coast

SAIGON, South Vietnam — (UPI) — Communist gunners shot down a U. S. Air Force Phantom jet off the coast of North Vietnam, then sank an amphibian rescue plane with mortar fire but an American helicopter braved the heavy shelling to rescue six of the eight crewmen involved, it was disclosed today.

A. U. S. military spokesman said the hair-raising incident occurred yesterday during one of 30 bombing missions by Navy and Air Force planes over the North.

He said the two-man crew of the Phantom F-4C, which was struck by conventional ground fire, bailed out into the sea two miles off the coast and 32 miles south of Thanh Hoa in the Panhandle region.

An Air Force HU-16 Albatross amphibian settled in the water near the two but mortars from nearby Hon Me Island scored direct hits on the lumbering rescue craft. The Albatross quickly sank.

A CARRIER-BASED helicopter then braved the North Vietnamese mortar barrage, swooped in and picked up six survivors. Two other Americans were lost, the U. S. spokesman said.

The American jet bombers ranged from the Panhandle — on the southeast coast north of the demilitarized zone separating the two Vietnams — far inland. They struck military and communications targets near Dien Bien Phu, 145 miles west of Hanoi, and destroyed 80 per cent of the Phu Qui barracks 40 miles north of the 17th Parallel demilitarized zone.

Pilots sighted one secondary explosion at Phu Qui which sent white smoke 1000 feet into the sky. The U. S. air armada also bombed and strafed other barracks, mortorized junks, ferry slips, highways and bridges.

In ground action, the Viet Cong today botched what was planned as their biggest Mekong Delta attack in weeks by throwing 1000 men against the wrong objective. Yesterday the Communists fumbled an ambush 325 miles northeast of Saigon and government troops killed at least 75 of them.

Auctioneer Here Found Bludgeoned to Death

Excise Tax Boost Due

Congress Approval Will Lift Revenue

WASHINGTON — (UPI) — Congress was expected today to swallow hard and go through with the politically distasteful election-year task of raising excise taxes to help provide $6 billion in extra revenues to fight the war in Vietnam.

Their action will bring the mounting costs of the war home to almost all Americans through higher telephone bills, higher costs for new cars and increased income tax withholding.

Both House and Senate were ready to give their final approval to the tax program, which Johnson had urged be pushed through Congress by today to get maximum benefit from its provisions. Following approval, it goes to the White House.

In addition to raising additional war revenues, the administration sought the bill to help combat inflation. Speculation was increasing, however, that Johnson would send a general tax increase bill later this year to further dampen inflationary trends.

The President's present proposal is aimed at bringing in $1.2 billion extra over the next 15 months by wiping out cuts in excise taxes on new cars and telephone calls that Congress approved only last year.

The remaining $4.8 billion would come from a "pay as you go" system of increased income tax withholding for higher income citizens and speeded up collection of corporate taxes. These would not involve increases but merely bring in tax money earlier than usual.

Congressional bill drafters worked on the bill until midnight last night to have it in shape. Johnson was given nearly all the funds he requested.

Enlistments May Delay Student Call

Larry Eugene Williams, 19, of RR 2, Old Henderson Road, sat quietly in City Court today while attorneys argued over whether he should be held as an accessory after the fact in the murder of Kenneth J. Sanders, 27, of 703 S.E. First Street, or as a material witness.

Another ADC Mother, Children on Relief Rolls

By FRED SIEVERS

Another mother has lost her monthly welfare income for having a "substitute father" in the house. As a result, she has ended up on township relief rolls.

"What else could we do?" asked Pigeon Township Trustee Robert Morrison when questioned about accepting the woman and her two children, both illegitimate, for township assistance.

"The law says the township trustee must provide for the poor and needy and somebody's got to feed those children," said Morrison.

It was the second case in three weeks where a mother has been removed from the Welfare Department's aid-to-dependent-children for allegedly living with a man not her husband.

[...] married but her husband lives elsewhere. She had been receiving $99 a month from the Welfare Department.

Meanwhile, three local agencies apparently are still at odds over what action, if any, should have been taken against the woman in the first case three weeks ago.

It involves a 26-year-old mother of five children removed from welfare rolls for allegedly living with a man. She, too, is receiving Pigeon Township assistance.

Suspect Faces Murder Charge

James Donald Stutsman, 27, of 1412 Olive, faced a preliminary murder charge this afternoon in City Court in the Sanders slaying case. Stutsman, who was arrested at midmorning in a restaurant at U.S. 41 North and Boonville Highway, was ordered held without bond for grand jury action.

By CHARLES SCHLEPER

A 27-year-old auctioneer was found dead shortly before 4 a.m. today in his downtown apartment, apparently killed by blows on the head from a flatiron.

Police said the motive appeared to be robbery.

Kenneth J. Sanders of 703 S.E. First Street was found face down on the floor of the bedroom in his two-room second floor apartment by police who were investigating a report that a man had been beaten at that address. Sanders was clad only in his underwear.

Deputy Coroner Ed Salisbury said Sanders died sometime between 2:30 and 3 a.m. He had four to six gashes on the back of his head, some as long as 2½ inches, Salisbury said. Sanders also had been struck in the eyes and nose, the deputy coroner added.

An autopsy to determine the exact cause of death was being conducted at Deaconess Hospital.

KENNETH SANDERS
Head Gashed

A SERVICE STATION attendant, Larry Eugene Williams, 19, of RR 2, Old Henderson Road, appeared in City Court today on a preliminary charge of being an accessory after the fact of murder.

A partial hearing was held this morning and Judge Wayne Kent took the case under advisement until this afternoon. Williams' attorney, Theodore Lockyear, objected to the charge saying, "It is an injustice that he is being held as an accessory. A material witness, yes, but not an accessory."

Detective Jess Julian, who questioned Williams, gave the following testimony in court today:

Williams said he went to Sanders' apartment about 3 a.m., wanting to borrow $3. As he approached an unidentified man, whom he did not know, came out and said Sanders wasn't home but he thought he knew where Sanders was if Williams would drive him there.

[...] Karges Jr., a personal friend, was on duty. He asked to have Karges meet him on the grocery parking lot.

Karges did and the policeman and Williams went to Sanders' apartment and found the body. They called Julian and later spent about an hour looking for the man Williams had seen at the building. They found the handkerchief where it had been thrown.

Julian asked that Williams be brought back to the police station for further questioning. It was there, while looking through police files, that Williams spotted a picture of the man he claimed to have met at the apartment and taken for the ride.

Williams described the man as white, about 23 years old, five feet nine inches, 180 pounds, with light brown hair, a light jacket and dark slacks.

Evansville Press, March 15, 1966. Auctioneer Ken Sanders was found bludgeoned to death in his apartment. James Stutsman was allowed to plead manslaughter for the brutal killing. *Evansville Vanderburgh Public Library*.

released. Williams's parents hired attorney Ted Lockyear, who stormed into the jail and demanded that his client be released and the charge be changed to material witness, as there was no evidence whatsoever that he in any way facilitated Sanders's murder. Judge Wayne Kent agreed.

A Hunch

Williams was tired after having been up all night, but he answered all the questions detectives asked of him, though his attorney made sure he made no incriminating statements. A detective asked him if he thought he could recognize the man he had driven around early that morning. "I believe I can. I saw him pretty clearly," he replied. The detective went into a file room and came out with a folder. In it was a black-and-white police photo of a handsome but rough-looking young man with dark hair.

"That's him; that's the man," Williams said, identifying a photograph of James Stutsman, twenty-seven, who had a minor police record. Asked later by reporters why he picked that particular photo to show Williams, the detective would say only that he acted on a "hunch."[58]

At about 10:30 a.m., acting on several anonymous tips after news had gotten out about Sanders's fate, two squad cars pulled up outside the small Chateau restaurant attached to a motel on U.S. 41, where Stutsman was having breakfast. Stutsman surrendered, and Williams was freed but ordered to remain in the city until further notice. Once in custody, Stutsman made a statement admitting to the beating of Sanders. Police did not immediately release the details of the statement.[59]

The autopsy showed Sanders had died of multiple skull fractures and his face had been crushed in, preventing him from breathing even if the skull wounds had not been fatal. Judge Kent called the grand jury into session on April 5, 1966. Stutsman was indicted for first-degree murder and felony murder in commission of a robbery in the death of Sanders, and bond was set at $50,000, an enormous sum in 1966. Stutsman was declared a pauper, and attorney Gary Gerling, a partner of Howard Sandusky, agreed to take the case for his defense. Immediately, a change of venue was sought and the case sent to Pike County, where Judge Lester Nixon would preside.[60]

After many delays, a trial date was set for October 3, 1966, in Petersburg, Indiana. On the first day of the trial, even before jury selection was to begin, deputy Vanderburgh County prosecutor James Kiely announced that a plea agreement had been reached. Stutsman, through his attorney, had agreed to plead guilty to manslaughter, which carried a two- to twenty-one-year sentence in the state prison system.

The prosecution released the original statement Stutsman had given police that had not been made public before. Stutsman said that he had met Sanders that day, March 14, 1966, and had been invited to his apartment for "a party." It was after they were alone, he said, that Sanders made "immoral advances" toward him. Stutsman said he beat Sanders to keep "him off of me," but he was so drunk he didn't realize what he had done. That was when he left the apartment and caught a ride with someone who was coming up the stairs, although he said he had little memory of the rest of the night.

Prosecutor Kiely explained, in the newspaper coverage, why he offered such a lesser charge for such a brutal murder. He said, "In cases where homosexuality is involved, it would be impossible to get a guilty verdict for first degree murder." Kiely gave the example of the 1963 murder of Rudolph Ziemer, where there were confessions and a solid trail of evidence and the jury still acquitted all three defendants, including the one who drove the car into the floodwaters that drowned Ziemer.[61]

Kiely said a plea of manslaughter would at least mean Stutsman would serve some time and carry the conviction the rest of his life. Stutsman was sentenced by Judge Nixon to two to twenty-one years in prison. Stutsman died at his home in Indianapolis, Indiana, in 2020 at the age of eighty-one.

The Gay Problem and the '60s in Evansville

Following the Sanders murder, the local newspapers began discussing homosexuality more openly, and never in a positive light. In the May 4, 1967 *Evansville Press*, reporter Ann Carey wrote a long piece on homosexuals and Evansville beginning with this paragraph:

> *A sports car pulls into the museum parking lot in Sunset Park on a warm night. Another car followed it. A slight man got out of the first car and disappeared over the levee. The driver of the other car, a man of medium build whose features are indistinguishable in the dark, follows him. Two homosexuals have made contact. The "Gay" life in Evansville is increasing, police say. They worry about it because it is spreading to more juveniles.*

This alarm sounded by the *Press* went on to describe what homosexuals are like: "It is often difficult to distinguish a homosexual. Some strive for he-men appearances and take karate and body building courses or wear leather jackets and ride motorcycles. One in Evansville was over 6 feet tall and weighed 255. Others look and act effeminate and wear elaborate hair styles and frilly fancy clothing."

Such language sounds quaint today, but in 1967, it was shocking to *Press* readers. The article went on to lament the lack of a "cure" for the illness that was homosexuality and the inability to prosecute most cases.

Police chief Darwin Covert told the reporter, "There isn't much you can do with two homosexual adults who get together willingly; you don't know it's going on unless one gets mad at the other and complains." Circuit Judge William Miller related that as long as he had been around (since

1965), only two men had been convicted of sodomy in his courtroom, although many more with such charges passed through. "You practically have to catch them in the act."

The article ended on a "positive" note for police: a new film had been obtained that "tastefully" warns parents about homosexuals and would be made available for groups to borrow showing the dangers of homosexuals in society.[62]

New Territory to Conquer

Nine years later, in 1976, the Evansville Police Department and the *Evansville Press* got together to do an exposé on "female Impersonators." Looking back from the vantage point of 2022, the story, written by Herb Marynell, a *Press* reporter (the afternoon newspaper of those days), is almost amusing had it not had such an impact on readers.

The headline read, "THE GAY LIFE—Female Impersonators pose a growing problem for police and courts." The story began on a dark downtown street in front of one of the many taverns that stood in the business district in those days. The reporter, riding in the patrol car, noted four women in long coats standing outside the tavern door. A policeman remarked, "That one is trying not to show us his face." Marynell was apparently surprised to learn the four women were males dressed in women's clothing.

The article explained, in remarkable detail, that a "medical" definition of a female impersonator would describe a male who dresses as a female to perform on a stage. They may or may not be homosexual, the article stated, based on descriptions from "psychological professionals." He went on to note that some are "gay" and some are "transsexuals" or one who "emotionally considers himself a woman and takes hormones to develop a bust." Some of them walk the streets, we read, to make money performing sex acts for men who may not know they are male.

A detective, unnamed in the piece, reports, "Evansville has become a center in Indiana for female impersonators. There are as many as 15 working the streets here." He said they were mostly Black, but there were a few white people as well.

The reporter found one person who didn't give a name but would talk about the current situation. Marynell listed the person as "a gay" or "the gay." He wrote:

> *The gay said most customers are white and contended half of them don't know the woman they are picking up is a male. "Evansville is just beginning to realize we are here," the gay said. "They are either going to have to cope with us or leave us alone. We are too many." The unnamed detective further bemoaned the situation where police were getting complaints from the "few active female street walkers we do have in Evansville and these impersonators are hurting their business."*

Even decades after city government stopped condoning a red-light district and regulating prostitution, female sex workers' complaints were noted.

The article ended by saying police and the courts were just beginning to try to figure out how to handle "transsexuals and homosexuals." Judge William Stephens was quoted as saying, "If I send a homosexual to jail, all I am doing is giving him new territory to conquer. It would cause disturbances in the prison system." The judge said he was looking at alternatives and that perhaps psychiatrists could suggest mental health agencies to refer "these people to" that would help.

Ironically, in this repressive period, gay men organized a cotillion at the historic Memorial Coliseum in downtown Evansville in the summer of 1972. Paul, one of the elders interviewed for this book, reported that people came from all over the tristate area, nearly two hundred as he recalled, some in formal drag, some in tuxedos. Paul was part of a short-lived group called the PAL Mattachine Society, named for the New York organization led by gay rights crusader Harry Hay. Also named for the bar Pal's Steak House, the organization sponsored the ball. The cotillion was held on June 3, 1972. There was a band, elegant décor and food. Paul said that there were security men hired, but they were unneeded that night; there was no disturbance at all. That formal ball was discussed for several years as an amazing event, but it never happened again.

It was during this period that several gay men bought homes in the historic district that had been cut up into apartments during World War II and began converting them back into single-family homes and in some cases reducing the number of units but renovating them. Many gay men and women still live in what is now the Preservation District. Although this trend is undocumented, it is well known in the city that part of the renovation and the fight to preserve historic homes came from an influx of LGBTQ people in the 1960s and 1970s.

In June 1977, Bob Hope came to the city to appear in a fundraiser for the children's section of the former Welborn Hospital. Along with Hope, singer

Protestors outside Vanderburgh Auditorium during the appearance of Anita Bryant, June 1977. *USI Archives/Dr. Stella Ress.*

Anita Bryant appeared and drew a small group of local LGBTQ activists protesting her virulent anti-gay campaign around the nation.

The aforementioned inflammatory article was written less than one year before the consenting adult legislation was passed in Indiana. It is a good reminder of the very negative attitudes a decade of unpunished murders of gay men encouraged and the dangerously marginalized environment LGBTQ+ persons in Evansville found themselves in just before the 1980s began.[63]

CHAPTER 8

A GIRL NAMED LAURA

1981

A seventy-year-old lesbian named Mallory remembers very clearly the beautiful girl named Laura whose vicious murder changed how the law in Evansville, Indiana, valued LGBTQ lives. Mallory said she and Laura Luebbehusen had known each other for years and enjoyed a deep friendship. Mallory's involvement in the lesbian community dated back to the early 1970s, when she started riding motorcycles with a group of young "rednecks," as she called them. Her group would ride into downtown Evansville to "whoop up some queers," which was not an unusual thing for young homophobic heterosexuals to do at that time.

Mallory said it was a summer night in probably 1971 or '72 when they roared down Second Street to an area behind the Old Post Office and Customs House, now restored to its original glory, where there was a small park created out of land recently cleared for urban renewal. This park was a cruising area for LGBTQ people. It was still illegal in Indiana to be queer. Once Mallory got to what they called "Sissies corner," she said a feeling came over her that indeed she belonged there and not with the group with whom she had arrived. Coming back later on her own, she began her own self-discovery of her true identity.

It was a few years later in the mid-1970s that she met Laura. Laura also loved motorcycles, and the two of them went on several long country rides together in southern Indiana and western Kentucky. Mallory may have had feelings for Laura, but apparently when Laura met a woman named Darlene, their rides stopped. Mallory saw Laura infrequently at a bar called the Cabaret, which was mainly a bar for lesbians, though a few men did hang out there. Mallory performed for several years as a male impersonator at various bars where such drag shows were permitted. "You had to be careful in those days," Mallory said. "You couldn't let the whole world know you were queer; you could lose your job, your family, hell, your life."

Her memories of Laura were especially painful when discussing what happened to her friend in February 1981.

Telephone

Number 1210 East Tennessee Street no longer exists in Evansville. The area was always a zone of industrial and commercial emergence. The houses along that side of the street were demolished a couple of decades ago. The repair shop across the street is still in operation, however. There's very little trace of the compact portion of the neighborhood that existed there. Where the house stood at 1210 is now a warehouse and operations center for Habitat for Humanity, an organization that builds houses for low-income families.

In the early months of 1981, one would have found a neat frame house at 1210 East Tennessee, with a small front porch and a black railing with two front doors. One door opened into the living room, and a second door opened into a front bedroom, a convention of homes built in the 1920s. The little house was owned by a local businessman and rented to Darlene Hooper, a divorced woman in her thirties who lived there with twenty-eight-year-old Laura Luebbehusen and a little cat.

Across the street was Tri State Repair, a business that makes repairs to all kinds of mechanical equipment. The business was in the process of remodeling some of its interior in the winter of 1980–81 and had employed some men for the job temporarily, one of whom was Thomas Schiro, a twenty-year-old who was living at the RESCUE halfway house on Kratzville Road, several miles from the little neighborhood.

Schiro had a long criminal history for someone only twenty years old. In the winter of 1980–81, he was serving time on work release for a robbery during which he had threatened to kill the victim. He had admitted to an alcohol problem and was attending Alcoholics Anonymous meetings, according to later testimony, but his enthusiasm was described by one counselor as "a show." He had a history of sexual violence, abusing women and peeping in windows at women in his childhood neighborhood.

He had a girlfriend who lived in Vincennes, Indiana, with her baby son. He was serving his current sentence on a work release permit, which allowed him to go to and from Tri State Repair only, but he was a frequent visitor at local bars as well before going back to the halfway house on Kratzville. The director of the RESCUE program later said they had no idea of the sexual violence in Schiro's past, or they never would have allowed him to be part of their program. But there he was in February 1981 anyway.

Laura was a delivery driver for the Charles Potato Chip company. In those days, the chip company delivered to homes and businesses around the city. She was home one afternoon and looking for her kitten that had gotten out of the house. She went across the street to ask the men working in the shop if they had seen the cat. They had not. But one of them did see the house she had come from. Schiro made a mental note of it.

On the evening of February 4, 1981, Laura left work and returned home around 6:30 p.m. She had apparently drawn a hot bath and was going to soak in the tub for a while. Darlene was gone, staying at her ex-husband's home for the night. Still good friends, Darlene and her ex had been on a ski trip with family. Twenty-eight-year-old Laura was alone in the house when there was a knock at the front door. Schiro introduced himself and reminded her of her visit looking for her cat. He said his car was not working and he needed to call a friend to come get him. She let him come in. He said later that he dialed a bogus number and pretended to talk to someone about coming to her house to pick him up.

A Mighty Struggle

When Darlene Hooper returned home on the morning of February 5, 1981, she and Michael discovered Laura's body, clothed only in a shirt and jacket that looked almost as though it had been pulled up to her throat. Her body had severe bite marks, and blood was spattered about the room. She was lying on her back just inside the front door, hands over her head. The rest of her clothing was nearby in a pile.

The first detective on the scene reported that there had been a mighty struggle in that house. From a front bedroom to the living room, things were broken and strewn everywhere. Apparently, Laura had fought against whomever did this to her in her last moments. The deputy coroner on the scene guessed that a steam iron nearby, badly broken in several places, had been used as a weapon to her head, but it appeared that her death was due to strangulation

Schiro admits 3 times to murder but not to police

By PATRICK W. WATHEN
and DAVID HULEN
Courier staff writers

Thomas Nicholas Schiro has confessed at least three times to last week's murder-rape of a 28-year-old Evansville woman — although not to the police.

Schiro, 20, formerly of Bicknell, Ind., was charged Tuesday in Circuit Court with murder, murder during the commission of rape and murder during the commission of criminal deviate conduct.

Schiro's arraignment in the death of Laura Jane Luebbehusen, who was found dead in her home at 1210 E. Tennessee St. last Thursday morning, was deferred until Thursday afternoon.

Records in the case and interviews with sources close to the investigation show that Schiro has confessed to Ken Hood, director of a halfway house where he lived, to his girlfriend in Vincennes, and to a fellow inmate at the Vanderburgh County Jail.

Prosecutor Jeffery Lantz said Tuesday he is waiting until the case file is more complete before deciding whether to seek the death penalty.

He said a decision should be made the first of next week.

Murder during the commission of a rape or criminal deviate conduct are among the charges for which the state may seek the death penalty.

Ordinarily, a suspect arrested in a felony is first taken to Misdemeanor Court to be preliminarily charged, but Lantz said his office found that sufficient evidence had been found to file formal charges.

Lantz also said that by not going through a pre-charge hearing, information in the case is limited, thus enabling authorities to obtain from future witnesses information they actually know "rather than what they read in the newspaper."

Last September, Schiro pleaded guilty to robbing a man on Jan. 26 and was sentenced to three years on the work-release program.

Allan Henson, director of the work-release program, said Schiro entered the program Sept. 30 and worked for a local restaurant and then a repair shop.

On Dec. 10, Schiro was ordered transferred from the County Jail to Rescue Inc.'s Second Chance halfway house at 3901 Kratzville Road.

(Hood said Schiro was not received at the halfway house until Dec. 22.)

"He was no problem to us," Henson said of Schiro. "He seemed genuinely concerned about his alcohol problems."

Henson said that while Schiro was in jail on the work-release program, he was sent to Alcoholics Anonymous meetings three times a week.

Two members of AA familiar with Schiro said he began attending meetings in early November and continued for the next two months. They said he attended Mondays, Tuesdays and Fridays and was an active participant at the meetings.

The AA members also said that Schiro's parents attended several meetings.

"He seemed to really care about overcoming his problem," said one acquaintance who also attended the meetings. "Almost too much. Sometimes it was like he was putting on a show."

The AA members said that when Schiro was transferred to the halfway house, he stopped coming to meetings.

Henson said that when he read Tuesday morning that Schiro had been arrested, "I was flabbergasted. ... It just didn't fit."

Henson described Schiro as "a little headstrong, but he wasn't a mean or argumentative individual."

Master Court Commissioner Maurice O'Connor, who sentenced Schiro in the robbery, said Schiro was insistent on receiving treatment for alcohol abuse.

O'Connor said the court had been receiving "glowing" reports on Schiro's progress from AA and a Vincennes psychologist Schiro was seeing.

Psychiatrists who examined Schiro in the robbery case reported to the court that Schiro was both competent to stand trial and sane.

Schiro told one doctor last March that he had had a drug problem and still had a drinking problem. He told the doctor his average daily alcohol consumption was a case of beer and a pint of whiskey.

Schiro has been a suspect in sex-related crimes in the Princeton, Ind.-Mount Carmel, Ill., area and in Knox

THOMAS SCHIRO
... Charged with murder

LAURA LUEBBEHUSEN
... Murder victim

County, Ind., but never was convicted.

A criminal deviate conduct charge is pending in Knox County, an official there said.

Schiro has a girlfriend, Mary Lee, and a 2-year-old child in Vincennes. Hood said Schiro had received weekend passes to go to Vincennes to visit Ms. Lee and the child.

Last Friday night, a Rescue staff member drove Schiro to the Greyhound bus station where Schiro caught a bus to Vincennes where he visited Ms. Lee, the child and his psychologist.

According to the probable cause affidavit filed with the court Tuesday, Ms. Lee told police that Schiro gave her the following account of the crime:

Schiro went to the 1210 E. Tennessee address late on Feb. 4 or early Feb. 5, knocked on the door and told the woman who answered that he had car trouble and needed to use her telephone to call for help.

Once inside, Schiro raped the women and then used an unspecified object to sexually assault her.

When the woman attempted to

(Continued on Page 3, col. 1)

Facility officials were unwarned of Schiro's past

By DAVID HULEN
and LARRY THOMAS
Courier staff writers

Officials of the Second Chance halfway house said Tuesday that Thomas Nicholas Schiro, charged in the murder of Laura Jane Luebbehusen, would never have been admitted if they had known he had been charged with sex-related crimes.

Schiro, 20, has been arrested in the past two years on charges involving rape and deviate criminal conduct in Illinois and in Knox County, Ind., although he was never convicted.

Schiro was referred to the Second Chance facility, 3901 Kratzville Road, by Master Circuit Court Commissioner Maurice O'Connor as part of a jail sentence for a robbery conviction here last year. Schiro had lived at the house since Dec. 22.

But Second Chance Director Ken Hood said Tuesday that a presentence report given to O'Conner and later passed on to the facility by court officials indicated that the robbery case was Schiro's first arrest, mentioned a drug and alcohol problem, but did not mention any previous clashes with the law.

"If we'd have known two months ago what we know today about him, we'd have never taken him," Hood said. "We don't take sex offenders. From what we saw, there was nothing to indicate to us that he was a potentially dangerous person."

Hood said the program's screening committee, which may reject persons referred by courts and prisons, normally relies on presentence investigation reports for background information on potential participants.

As a result of Schiro's arrest, Hood said, the program will begin running FBI checks on all persons referred to the program.

It was the first major incident involving a resident of the halfway house, but Hood and others said they are concerned the incident could set off a new wave of attacks on the sometimes-controversial facility, opened in October 1977 as a stepping stone between prison and society.

"Really, it's the worst thing that could happen to us," Hood said. "I can understand the community reaction. There's a need for concern and a need for questions to be asked. I welcome that. But I think it's very important for people to look at all the facts before

KEN HOOD
... Unaware of man's past

making a judgment about the Second Chance house or condemning the program."

The facility, funded through government grants, private support and rent paid by residents, currently houses 34 offenders who are serving sentences for a variety of crimes. They range from former inmates of federal prisons to first-time felony convicts, and the time they spend in the program ranges from several months to more than a year.

Inmates in the program are required to hold outside jobs. Those with good records are allowed to leave the facility in the evening and weekends, although all residents are required to sign in and out, and cannot leave after 11 p.m. Any major rule violation results in an inmate being sent back to prison, or back to court for resentencing, Hood said.

"It's not a punishment-oriented program, and it has been successful," Hood said. "The majority of people who have gone through here are leading productive lives."

When the halfway house was opened, there was considerable opposition from residents of the neighborhood, located just west of North Park shopping center. The Kratzville Road location was chosen after a proposal to locate it at 318 Walnut St. was scrapped after some city officials argued the house would be too close to bars and other places that offenders shouldn't frequent.

The neighborhood around the halfway house consists primarily of older but well-kept homes and several newer apartment developments. The Buena Vista Day Care Center is located on the same property as the halfway house, and the Holiday Home Health Care Center, a convalescent home, is around the corner at 1201 Buena Vista Road.

Tuesday night, some residents of the area said the arrest of Schiro has made

(Continued on Page 3, col.1)

Evansville Courier, February 10, 1981. The murder of Laura Luebbehusen changed how juries valued LGBTQ lives. Schiro was convicted of capital murder. *Evansville Vanderburgh Public Library.*

by some marks on her neck and throat. Landlord Louis Rothchild had rented the house to Hooper in January. The two women had moved in only three weeks earlier. Laura had told friends she had been living near downtown, but her work delivery truck had been vandalized and she had been concerned about several rapes that had occurred nearby. She moved here to feel safer.

Laura's personal car, a 1974 Toyota, was found about a quarter of a mile from the house a few days later, and police combed it for clues but found very little. The maroon car was parked in front of an apartment building on North Fulton Avenue. Neighbors did not recall seeing anyone get in or out of it. Friends the police spoke with said it was not unusual for Laura to loan her car to them while she was working because she drove a Charles Chips delivery van on shift.

Her funeral was on Monday, February 9, in her hometown of Ferdinand, Indiana, about an hour north of Evansville.[64]

Confessions

Ken Hood, the director of the Second Chance Halfway House for ex-offenders, became suspicious about one of his inmates when he learned Laura's car had been found very near his facility. He checked the night sign-in sheets, where a case worker supervises work-release inmates signing in and out. Schiro had not signed in on the evening of February 5 and had called from Tri State Repair earlier to say he was working late. A supervisor drove to the shop on East Tennessee and saw men working inside. He did not stop. Hood also remembered Schiro had been allowed a pass to travel to Vincennes to see his girlfriend, Mary Lee, on the weekend of February 8. Schiro was back in the center on Monday, February 9, the day of Laura Luebbehusen's funeral.

While in Vincennes, Schiro told Mary Lee a bizarre story about a girl in Evansville whom he had just killed. He said he had seen her once and knew where she lived and took a chance she'd be home alone when he knocked. He used the story about needing the phone. Once inside, he asked to use the restroom. He came out with his genitals exposed and told her not to worry because he was gay but had bet someone he could "make it with a woman." Though she struggled, he said he managed to rape her more than once and got her to drink some wine trying to calm her down. He drank too much and passed out for a bit. When he came to, Laura had dressed and was going out the door, saying she was going to look for her girlfriend and he should leave.

He got up and started beating her with a metal steam iron and whatever else he could find and finally strangled her. He told Mary that he violated Laura's corpse and then left, taking her car. A day later, Mary called Evansville authorities to report what Schiro had told her.

Back at the halfway house late in the evening on Monday, February 9, someone had left water running in a second-floor bathroom, and it ran over the sink and caused wetting of the downstairs ceiling. Some of the other men blamed it on Schiro. Hood took Schiro into a room and questioned him about it, but he denied any knowledge of the water faucet. Hood suggested a lie detector. Schiro became nervous then and said, "You mean about the water or what?"

Hood asked him about the maroon Toyota that had been found nearby that belonged to the murdered girl. "Did you drive that car?" Schiro hung his head and said, "Yeah."

"Did you kill that girl?"

"Yeah, I did." Schiro told him about the girl he'd met when she was looking for her lost kitten, asking to use the phone and then getting drunk and killing her. Hood took Schiro to police headquarters and turned him in for killing Luebbehusen.

Don't Come In

Schiro's trial was moved to the small Brown County town of Nashville, a scenic little place dotted with early twentieth-century buildings housing antique shops and other specialty stores. The community hardly took note of the dramatic trial taking place in its courthouse in September 1981. It was one of the most lurid trials in the history of southern Indiana. Laura Luebbehusen's killer was so depraved and such a sociopath that it was difficult to read the news from the trial.

The prosecuting attorney, Jerry Atkinson, questioned each potential juror with a query that echoed back to the three murders of gay men in Evansville in the 1960s. As each Brown County resident took the stand to be vetted, Atkinson would ask, "Do you think it is less wrong to kill a homosexual person than it is anyone else?" Each of the eighty-five prospective jurors responded "no." Atkinson warned them that they would see disturbing photographs and hear graphic testimony about bizarre sexual practices. No one blanched. A jury of six men and six women was seated.

The first day of the trial, September 5, 1981, the defense attorney portrayed Schiro as a victim of exposure to pornography at the age of eight or nine. He became addicted to it later, peeping in windows and masturbating outside. He hanged cats. He was responsible for raping nineteen women during his teen years, becoming increasingly mentally unbalanced. The unfortunate intersection of his demented mind and pretty Laura Luebbehusen occurred because of a lost cat and an opportunity. A girl home alone, trusting a man who helped her look for a lost pet that cold day in January.

A parade of witnesses testified for both the defense and the prosecution.

A fellow inmate of Schiro's in the Vanderburgh County jail testified that Schiro confessed his crime while they were cellmates, shortly after his arrest. Schiro told inmate David Parrish that he "didn't remember much about the killing because he'd taken so many drugs and drank so much whiskey that it all ran together."

The defense attorney, Michael Keating, who claimed he had received death threats for acting as legal counsel for Schiro, tried to present a case that mitigated the circumstances. Laura had first welcomed Schiro into her home that night, giving him drinks and company and sex. His killing of her was the result of forces in his mind that he could not control, which eventually led him to commit necrophilia, raping her corpse after he'd murdered her by beating and strangulation.

For her part, Schiro's girlfriend told the court how he was an abusive man and how during their association he did very bizarre things like confessing he'd fallen in love with a female mannequin in a clothing store window. Once, the store put a different color wig on the statue, and he went inside to complain about it. Schiro had confessed to a psychologist that he liked to hold Mary's one-year-old under running water until he passed out and then revive him.

The testimony that was the hardest to hear was that of Hooper, Laura's lover. She testified to the nature of her relationship with Laura and was forced to identify and discuss the use of several sex devices that Schiro had stolen from the house and discarded in Vincennes. Police had recovered them, and the prosecution entered them as evidence.

"She would not have encouraged him," said Hooper. "The thought of sex with men was repulsive to her. She was a lesbian." With that, Laura's identity was there for all the world to judge. The piece of evidence that moved witnesses the most was a hand-scribbled note on a piece of paper soaked in blood that Laura had written quickly. It read, "Darlene please don't come in I've called the police." One of her last earthly acts was to save her lover from possibly meeting the same fate. No one knows at what point she wrote the note, but it never made it to the other side of the bedroom door entrance to the house they shared.

Atkinson's question to the jurors finally took on some meaning, much like Howard Sandusky's questions to jurors in the trial of Rudolph Ziemer nearly twenty years earlier. But this time, the answer was different. On Saturday night, September 12, 1981, the jury returned a verdict of guilty of murder in the commission of a rape and later recommended the death penalty. Schiro is in prison still.[65]

CHAPTER 9

REVEREND HARRY CHARLES KEETON

1984

From the earliest days, Evansville's Sunset Park, which lies between Riverside Drive and the Ohio River bank, has been a cruising ground for homosexual men. During the decades when homosexuality was illegal, being arrested there took on much greater significance than after legalization in 1977. Evansville police frequently went back and forth in their enforcement of the closing hours of the park. Sometimes an officer would drive through and just tell people to move on. Other times, an officer who held particularly homophobic views would abuse a gay man found wandering there at night. Sometimes police would arrest the men for loitering or some other charge.

The Evansville gay community, which by 1984 was fairly established if not always public or out, had several bars, a few people in fairly high positions in the city and a definite network of news-sharing "tea," as we call it. It was no surprise to the LGBTQ community, then, on a chilly November morning that someone had been shot to death in the wee hours in the dark parking lot next to the tennis courts. What did surprise queer people was that it was a probable closeted Episcopal priest from southern Illinois.

Even with an open culture, closeted men still preferred the darkness of night and out-of-the-way places to find sex, love or companionship. These places in Evansville could be dangerous, as the Reverend Harry Charles Keeton discovered in the early morning hours of November 30, 1984.

The Evansville COURIER

Serving the Tri-State since 1845

FOUNDED JAN. 7, 1845; VOL. 140—NO. 284 | EVANSVILLE, IND., SATURDAY, DECEMBER 1, 1984 | 25 CENTS | FINAL EDITION

Photo courtesy of the McLeansboro Times-Leader

The Rev. Harry Charles Keeton at his McLeansboro, Ill., church

Priest shot three times in the head

By ROD SPAW
and JARI JACKSON
Courier staff writers

An Episcopal priest found dead in his car early Friday at Sunset Park had been shot three times in the right side of the head, an autopsy revealed later Friday.

Deputy Coroner William Sandefur said the Rev. Harry Charles Keeton, 53, of McLeansboro, Ill., was shot at close range.

Sandefur said bullets recovered during the autopsy were not easily identifiable, but he said Keeton probably was shot with a small caliber weapon.

Sandefur said Keeton also was shot through the right hand as if he had tried to protect himself.

Keeton was dressed in jogging pants, buttoned shirt, a windbreaker and tennis shoes, police said.

Evansville Police Capt. Charles Berlin said detectives believe Keeton was shot as he sat on the driver's side of the vehicle. The body was found slumped toward the passenger side of the 1983 Oldsmobile Cutlass, which was found at 2:30 a.m. Friday in the parking lot of Sunset Park off Waterworks Road.

Berlin said Keeton may have been robbed, but police were not certain. He said no weapon was found.

The body was discovered by officers Tom Harvey and Randy Dennis during a routine patrol of the park, according to police.

Keeton, originally from Oklahoma City, was vicar for two small Episcopal missions in southern Illinois — St. James Church in McLeansboro and St. Stephens Church in Harrisburg. A vicar in the Episcopal Church is a priest who serves as a representative of the diocese to a congregation that is not formally an established church.

> "He told us he spent time in Evansville and St. Louis, but why and with whom I don't know. I'm as much in the dark as anyone."

Keeton lived in an apartment in the two-story parish hall adjacent to St. James and alternated Sunday services between the two congregations, according to church members. Berlin said city detectives went to McLeansboro and Harrisburg Friday to interview acquaintances and church members.

"We're just trying to track his activities yesterday (Thursday) and determine whom he might have been coming over to see," Berlin said.

Police said Keeton had checked into the Executive Inn Thursday, but they did not know what had brought him to Evansville. Church members said Keeton was known to travel to

(Continued on Page 3, col. 3)

Evansville Courier, November 30, 1992, on the murder of Reverend Harry Keeton in Sunset Park. *Evansville Vanderburgh Public Library.*

FOUR MINUTES

Evansville police officers driving along Riverside Drive were on a routine circuit of the downtown about 2:30 a.m. early Friday, November 30, 1984. The Sunset Park entrance off Waterworks Road wound around to a parking lot near an older set of clay tennis courts mainly used by high school tennis teams to practice and by residents of the nearby Riverside Historic neighborhood. The park officially closed every night at 11:00 p.m., but many gay men continued to cruise the park after closing time. Police sometimes watched for them, as technically they were violating city ordinance.

Officers on patrol that morning noticed a parked car, a newer Oldsmobile Cutlass, parked next to the tennis court. The car was not running, nor was it damaged that they could see. A policeman exited the patrol car and shined his flashlight into the driver's side window. Lying across the front bench seat was a man dressed in a maroon jogging suit with a white shirt; his head was covered with blood.

Officers called for an ambulance and backup, but the man was dead. It appeared to the officers and medical team that he had been shot just minutes earlier. All wounds, including one through his right hand, were fresh and still bleeding. The deputy coroner estimated the shots entered his body less than four minutes before the officers entered the park.[66]

His wallet was lying on the ground nearby, identifying him as the Reverend Harry Charles Keeton. The pathology report showed he had been shot four times—three small-caliber bullets to the head at close range and one in his right hand as he apparently tried to shield himself. The police said at the time that they "suspected homosexual activity" but were never specific about those details, even later when a suspect was identified. The coroner concurred with the first officers on the scene that he had been shot just three or four minutes before he was found.[67] The gay community suspected that police didn't fully discuss their sexual theory because of the desire not to encourage imitation.

Police began searching for clues as to why Keeton was in Evansville. He had been the clergyman for two separate parishes in Illinois: St. James in McLeansboro and St. Stephens in Harrisburg. Originally from Oklahoma, Keeton obtained a degree in psychology and established a counseling practice in New York City for a time. His bishop, Donald Hultstrand, in Illinois, told police that Keeton was hoping to establish a similar psychotherapy practice in Illinois but would soon have gone back to New York for additional education.

Reporters began combing through Keeton's life in Illinois. Two McLeansboro church committee members told the newspapers that Keeton "liked to travel to both Evansville and St. Louis although he never told anyone here why." His aged parents lived in Oklahoma City, and they had his remains shipped there for funeral and burial.

Potato Chips

There were few clues in Keeton's murder. He had checked into the Executive Inn, a downtown hotel that used to stand between Fifth and Sixth Streets at Walnut, at about 4:55 p.m. on November 29 and was killed at 2:30 a.m. the following morning. There was no one in Evansville who could help trace

Keeton's activities in between those hours. No one reported seeing him at a restaurant. Bartenders at the local gay bars were questioned, but no one recognized his photographs as a patron that night.[68]

Through 1985, the newspapers occasionally would print a story about the Keeton murder, as it was the one unsolved killing from 1984. Only one other witness talked about the case, and he could not completely identify Keeton. Dave Paddock told detectives he had driven through Sunset Park early on November 30, at 1:30 a.m. Paddock said that he saw a newer Oldsmobile and an older gold 1971 or 1972 Buick parked next to it. There were two men in the newer car: an older man with a large build and a younger, thinner Black man sitting in the passenger seat. Paddock didn't see anything else and went on his way. It wasn't unusual to see cars there and people getting in and out of them after the park closed.

Police had one other clue. In Keeton's hotel room, there was a small bit of trash lying about, specifically a potato chip bag presumably from a hotel vending machine that had some fingerprints on it, and there was a small plastic bucket in the back of Keeton's car that had a bloody fingerprint. None of the prints matched any in their database, however.

On Friday, January 4, 1986, a tip from an informant led police to Westville, Indiana, and to a young man named Patrick Collins. Collins was incarcerated at the Westville Maximum Security Penitentiary for carrying a handgun without a permit. A cellmate told authorities Collins had related to him that he had "killed a homosexual" in a park and then raided his hotel room for money and other valuables. The FBI matched Collins's fingerprints to those on the chip bag and the bucket. Collins was arrested on felony murder charges when his fingerprints matched those on both items found in Keeton's hotel room and Cutlass.[69]

Collins denied he had killed Keeton. He told police and, later, a jury that he and a female companion happened on the car parked in Sunset Park and found Keeton already dead. He admitted taking the wallet's contents and the hotel room key (they were traditional metal keys in 1984) and going to the Executive Inn room where Keeton was staying to see if there was anything of value there. He didn't deny eating a bag of chips there either.

Collins's brother also told police his brother had come home the morning of the killing and told him that he had "killed a queer in Sunset Park" and needed to leave town, so he needed money.

Trial

Collins went on trial for Keeton's murder in May 1986. Vanderburgh Superior Court judge William Stephens presided, and deputy prosecutor Stan Levco represented the people. Glen Grampp was the attorney for the defense. During the jury selection, those old echoes of past jury trials drifted into the modern courtroom of 1986. "Do you feel a violent crime is more, or less, worthy of punishment if the victim was homosexual?" jurors were asked. All of the prospective jurors agreed that violence against homosexuals was just as worthy of punishment.

There were several days of testimony in the case, in which Collins's brother changed his earlier statements that Patrick told him he had killed a homosexual in the park and needed to leave town. Collins himself danced around a story about getting blood on his hands by finding the body and touching a bucket while looking for a cloth to wipe himself. Prosecutor Levco made the statement that probably sealed the case.[70]

Looking at the jury, he said, "Mr. Collins here has 24 different lies in his statement. The one truth was that he said he liked to beat up gays." Collins was convicted of murder but not of robbery, which saved him from the death penalty. He was sentenced to eighty years in the state penitentiary. His attorneys appealed, but the Indiana Supreme Court affirmed the conviction in April 1988.[71]

Brian Russell and Norm Ellerbrook

On September 3, 1993, Norm Ellerbrook, sixty-four, was at his home in Warrenton, Indiana, where he lived alone. He was the head chef at the Executive Inn in downtown Evansville. He was a large man, weighing nearly four hundred pounds, and he was gay. He had many friends in the local LGBTQ community. Sometime that night, he was brutally murdered in his home. Sheriff's deputies reported that the downstairs of the home was covered in blood and it appeared that he had struggled with his killer in nearly every room of the house before succumbing to the many stab wounds on his body and subsequent loss of blood.

Several days later, Ellerbrook's car was found parked on a side street near Ol' Sweig's tavern at 1200 First Avenue. The old brick tavern was a neighborhood favorite, but no one in the area recalled seeing the car being parked or how long it had been there. One neighbor was particularly concerned about Ellerbrook's car being found where it was.[72]

Brian Russell, forty-four, lived above his used furniture and appliance store at 1201 First Avenue. He was also a large man and known in the gay community. He was the quintessential used furniture salesman: he wore flashy jewelry and always carried a large amount of cash, mistrusting banks. His store was well kept, and he had a fair reputation for business.

He had been friends with Ellerbrook and was worried enough to talk to police about it. He said to one detective that it "freaked me out" that Ellerbrook's car was parked across the street from where he lived and worked. They had been good friends, and in his mind, whoever killed Ellerbrook might know about his friendship with the murdered man. Police at the time did not suspect any connection but urged Russell to be cautious.

On March 1, 1995, Brian Russell's father was worried because his son hadn't come downstairs to work, nor had he answered his calls for twenty-four hours. Clifford Russell came upstairs and found his son's body, fully clothed, at the foot of his bed. He had been stabbed multiple times. Some of his jewelry was missing, as was his wallet. When police came, one of them remembered Russell had expressed concern when his friend's car had been found across the street two years earlier.[73]

You Don't Want to Do That, Tim

Shannon Farber, Timothy Farber's wife, confided in a friend that her husband, whom she had just asked to leave their home, had confessed that he had killed Russell. Farber had an off-and-on sexual relationship with Russell and had worked for him periodically. The friend reported the conversation to the authorities. Police confronted Shannon Farber, and she admitted that her husband had indeed confessed. She agreed to wear a hidden microphone and go talk to Farber, who was picketing with his union near Main and Sycamore Streets downtown. In that recorded conversation, he again said that he had killed Russell and robbed him of money and jewelry. He was immediately arrested.[74]

Farber expressed remorse at that point and led police to the small lake where he had placed Russell's wallet, rings and other items into a coffee can and tossed it into the water. Farber said he had gone to Russell's apartment to ask for a loan and became enraged when Russell said no. Farber said he turned to leave, but in a moment of rage, he turned and pulled his large knife. Russell said to him, "You don't want to do that, Tim." Farber stabbed him in the neck. Russell fell to the floor, and Farber sat on the bed listening to him moan and kept stabbing his body to quiet him down until he finally died.

Farber was convicted of murder and sentenced to life without parole. He appealed the sentence, but it was affirmed in 1998 by the Indiana Supreme Court. Ellerbrook's murder was never solved, but police speculated the killer was Farber.

By the 1990s, juries gave the same weight to the life of a homosexual (self-identified or perceived) as a heterosexual. The long fight for justice had come full circle in Evansville.[75]

CHAPTER 10

THE PARTY

AIDS AND THE CITY

In May 1981, the *Sunday Courier and Press*, led by the rather bold editor Judy Clabes, ran a long interview think piece by a young journalist, Joycelyn Winnecke, whose brother eventually became mayor, about LGBTQ Evansville. In keeping with the early 1980s culture, it was titled "Gays Existing in a Straight World." The focus was mainly on white, cisgendered gay men, although Winnecke did interview a lesbian for her perspective.

The article was designed to, and for a time did, change perceptions some Evansville residents had about their mostly closeted queer neighbors. None of the subjects of the story allowed their names to be used. One of the men was married to a woman and, of course, wanted his identity protected, but all of them agreed that if they were identified, their lives would change for the worse: loss of job, loss of friends and potentially family and even becoming the target of violence.

That Sunday morning, groups of Evansville queer families of choice gathered over brunch to read the piece. Some knew one or two of the subjects, as they had told friends that they were in the story. Other groups tried to figure out the names like a parlor game. But overall, it was a positive move, an attempt to bring sensitivity to a long marginalized and targeted group.[76]

Gays were becoming more visible. You could spot someone who more or less looked gay at the booming disco clubs like Funky's located in the southwestern corner of downtown or Good Time Bobby's, a dressier, more upscale dance club on the East Side. The gay party crowd would start a Saturday evening at one of the straight clubs, have a few drinks and mingle with friends who didn't care about their sexuality and dance a while. At 11:00 p.m. or so, if inclined, the gays and occasionally a straight couple or two would head to the Swinging Door, the open bright and booming gay bar on the West Side, located across from a bottle cap factory on Maryland Street.

There, groups would mingle with drag queens who performed at midnight for tips in a one-hour or so lip-synch show. Then at 1:00 a.m., at least in 1981, the DJ, a tall, good-looking man named Mike Wilson, would play a current bar favorite like Cher's "Take Me Home" or Lipps Inc. "Funkytown" that would get everyone out on the mirrored, flashing lighted dance floor immediately. Singles would try to pair up for the night or, if dating already, would leave at the 3:00 a.m. closing time. Wilson would play Lawrence Welk's closing theme to get people out.

For others who didn't want to stop the party, occasionally a gay couple everyone knew, named Brian and Earl, would throw an "after bar party" at a small house on the southeast side, 1313 Crabapple Circle. The diehards would crowd into the little house and continue the fun until the sun started to rise. If you were on the right list, huge outdoor parties were held at the beginning and end of summer by two gay male couples on their large properties in suburban Evansville. At a historic home in town, a gay male couple held viewing parties for the popular *Dynasty* TV series that turned into weekly gatherings even after the show was canceled; years later, they watched *Queer as Folk*. For younger cisgendered gay men at least, it was an affirmation that one "belonged" in a time of marginalization. They were short-lived halcyon days.

It was the culmination of the liberation movement nationwide and its fledgling beginnings toward some kind of organized queer life in our hometown.

About a month after Winnecke' s article appeared, a mysterious disease began impacting gay men on the coasts. A "gay cancer" was manifesting itself in a rare form of cancerous cells called Kaposi sarcoma. These men were dying of it in their thirties. Queer Evansville read these beginning stories with some interest but no real dread. At first.

Alarm Bells

On April 5, 1983, the *Evansville Courier* ran a story on page 24 (the back page) about the local Red Cross offices stating that as of that date, they would ask all potential blood donors to "screen themselves" before donating blood. The article stated that of the 1,200 known cases (none in Evansville), only one transmission of the mysterious illness affecting Haitian immigrants and homosexual men had been the cause of an infection. "We will not be in a position of asking someone's sexual preference," said Fred Cottrell, then the director of the local office.[77]

By 1983, Evansville was aware and conscious of the disease that was affecting gay men on the coasts and at that time was tied to immigrants from the economically devastated island of Haiti. There was no widespread panic in the city either from the LGBTQ community (although discussions of the deadly disease were taking place in the bars and other places gay people tended to congregate) and certainly none in the community at large. AIDS, recently named for its clinical term Acquired Immune Deficiency Syndrome, was still the fodder of late-night talk show jokes.

On April 17, 1983, the *Sunday Courier and Press* published a lengthy article about the prevalence of sexually transmitted diseases, AIDS being one that only "certain high-risk populations are impacted by," and defined one group as "promiscuous homosexuals." This definition seemed to take hold as a reason not to be concerned. The article quoted Phyllis Schlafly, then the leader of the right-wing wave sweeping the Reagan-dominated national landscape, as saying the diseases now manifesting themselves were the obvious result of the sexual liberation of the 1970s.[78]

News about AIDS began to accelerate. In a May 19, 1983 article, the *Evansville Courier* reported that cases of the disease were being reported in heterosexual women who were infected by men who carried the virus; thus, the article implied, the disease could affect the general population. As 1983 turned into 1984, the pace and number of newspaper stories grew exponentially. There seemed to be an AIDS article every day. The three local TV news programs began featuring medical professionals discussing the potential impact on Evansville even though the first local case had not been reported yet.[79]

In November 1984, an article appeared in the *Courier* stating that in 1984, AIDS cases nationally were up 75 percent over 1983, and more than two-thirds of the patients who contracted the illness before 1983 were already dead. The Atlanta CDC official interviewed said it would be unlikely for those expanding numbers to continue, however, ten years into the future. Throughout 1984, mainline evangelical churches began featuring discussions of AIDS in sermons and advertising the topic in their Sunday liturgies. These sermons described the illness as the natural result of homosexuality and its sin.[80]

It was February 20, 1985, when the first area AIDS case was reported. A man who listed his home address as Henderson, Kentucky, was admitted to St. Mary's Hospital in Evansville for symptoms of serious infection. When he tested positive for the AIDS virus, he was sent to the Indiana University Hospital in Indianapolis, where the diagnosis was confirmed. Dr. Jane Hoops, then Vanderburgh County health officer, said that rumors about a death from AIDS in Evansville were false and this was the only area case officially diagnosed.[81]

In July 1985, twin stories caused widespread discussions about AIDS in TV news, newspapers and office breakrooms. Famed actor Rock Hudson was reportedly dying of AIDS after returning to the United States from France (he died on October 2), and a Kokomo, Indiana seventh-grader named Ryan White was being barred from returning to his school because the child suffering with hemophilia had contracted the virus in a blood transfusion. There were debates about both stories, with many agreeing that the child should be kept away from his classmates. Letters to the editors of both daily Evansville newspapers covered all sides of the argument and were on the rise. Writers called for quarantining of all male homosexuals, returning to the old sodomy laws; others wrote to seek compassion for the suffering and dying and called for increases to funding research for a cure. It was a heated battle that had just begun.

In the Sunday, September 22, 1985 issue of the *Sunday Courier and Press*, a reporter covered an advertised workshop hosted by the fledgling Tri State Alliance of Gays and Lesbians and the Red Cross that had been held at the Universal Unitarian Church the day before. Yvon Mabrey, the Tri State Alliance's founder, expressed disappointment that only twelve people turned out, but she felt the meeting was only the beginning of an educational process that had to happen.[82]

John Fowler, a co-chair of the group, reported that the "gay community is upset. They are modifying how they behave in bars. If someone is known to be promiscuous, most are shying away from them and using other means of meeting people, like placing newspaper ads." The gay community was worried, Mabrey was quoted as saying, about increasing hostility from the city at large. Homophobia had a new excuse. Dr. Bernard Lourie, a communicable disease specialist at Welborn Hospital, reported that there were at least three known cases of AIDS in Evansville at that time and three suspected cases, although none of them was contracted here. The national count at that point was up to twenty thousand.

In that September 22, 1985 issue, the *Sunday Courier and Press* encouraged a "reader referendum" on whether to prohibit children infected with the AIDS virus from attending school. The results of that referendum were published the following Sunday, September 29, with some commentary from readers. They showed that 82 percent of respondents favored keeping children with AIDS out of the public schools. One respondent wrote, "No child with a communicable disease should be allowed in a classroom with other children."[83]

Throughout 1985, newspaper advice columnists published letters from anxious parents, concerned spouses and others asking myriad questions about the disease that was killing nearly everyone it touched. Columnists like Ann Landers and Dear Abby preached compassion, concern and honesty among couples about the topic. One mayoral candidate in Houston, Texas, was heard to say he recommended "shooting the queers" as a cure. He raised an additional $70,000 for his campaign immediately after that news broke.

On June 18, 1986, during a campaign stop in Evansville, Rick McIntyre, the Republican candidate for the Eighth District congressional seat, declared that he would "send a letter to the Reagan administration that part of any assistance for AIDS research must contain language that calls for condemnation of homosexual acts." He said that while there were fewer than one hundred actual cases in Indiana, it was an issue people were "frightened about," and he believed condemning homosexuality was part of the cure for the spread.[84]

His opponent, incumbent congressman Frank McCloskey, a former mayor of Bloomington, Indiana, defended the five-point plan the Health and Human Services Department had recently issued about AIDS but did not refer to homosexuality in his comments. McIntyre lost the election in November despite President Ronald Reagan visiting Evansville on his behalf.

During the summer of 1986, a team of social service professionals in Evansville—led by Larry Rowland of the Southwest Indiana Mental Health Center and Jane Hoops with the Vanderburgh County Health Department, among others—united to provide a framework to help anyone diagnosed with AIDS. Rowland stated in a July 6, 1986 news story that people diagnosed with cancer have a built-in support network that takes the patient's role in consideration of treatment and its outcome. A person diagnosed with AIDS may find his or her support network pulled away out of fear or bias. Local victims—by then there had been three deaths—were between the ages of twenty-five and forty-nine, far younger than most people who become ill with a fatal illness, and required end-of-life care much earlier than normal and the psychosocial needs therein.[85]

During the summer and fall of 1986, county health officials called for the creation of a health education person to promote education among affected/impacted communities as to how to avoid the AIDS virus. At the same time, the ferocity of letters to the editors of the newspapers increased with references to God's punishment for sin and sexual liberation and the biblical stories of Sodom and Gomorrah.

During the summer's local government budget processes, the city under Mayor Michael Vandeveer refused to put additional funds into the city budget to pay for an AIDS educator in the Health Department budget, which was split between city and county administrations. The county council, the fiscal body of the county, advised they would fund the position themselves.

On April 12, 1987, the formation of the AIDS Resource Group was announced by co-chairs Richard Franz, a counselor with Stepping Stone, an addiction clinic, and Patty Loehr, a social worker/mental health therapist. Together with a variety of others, they formed the consortium to try to coordinate all the types of services a person diagnosed with AIDS would need to navigate his or her treatment and remaining lifetime dealing with the incurable illness. The closeted nature of the LGBTQ community in the Evansville area posed a significant challenge, so the organizers would have to resort to many unorthodox methods of communication and outreach. The primary concern was twofold: education of those at risk and connecting victims of the illness to care and monetary benefits they might be able to receive. The organization still exists today.[86]

The Dance

When Myreon Taylor graduated from Evansville's Central High School in 1966, all he could think about was leaving his hometown. Though born in Canada, he grew up here from childhood on. He said in an interview in 1984, as he was taking on the job of senior jazz and tap instructor with the Evansville Dance Theater, "There weren't a lot of opportunities for a singer/actor/dancer in Evansville in the late 1960s, especially one who was Black. Every day was a day waiting to leave." Indeed, he did leave to earn a degree in theater from Indiana State University at Terre Haute and went on to a career in dance both in Chicago and studying at the Harlem Dance Theater of New York after a stint in the U.S. military. He could be seen in two off-Broadway plays and the Bill Murray film *Stripes*, and he performed in Europe and around the world.

Then his mother died, and he came home to, as he put it, "rest a minute and reflect." He was fresh from operating his own dance company in Louisville, Kentucky, for five years before coming back to his hometown. He was surprised to find a functioning dance company, led in those days by Jean Allenby. She immediately hired him to dance, train and choreograph. Evansville audiences who attended ballet and other dance performances became very familiar with the tall, lithe Black dancer who could make the most complicated moves seem easy and routine.[87]

In 1985, Taylor won rave reviews for a modern jazz and ballet combination of his own creation. His work, *A Haze Suspended*, blended modern ballet with what was then the new phenomenon of break dancing, usually performed by urban youth on streets and in clubs. Bill Greer, the arts reviewer, glowed with praise for what he termed genius interpretations of everyday city life through the movements of dance. Taylor seemed to have boundless energy and creativity.[88]

METRO

FINAL EDITION

Tireless AIDS fighter loses final battle

Choreographer and dancer dies

By LINDA NEGRO and ROGER McBAIN
Courier staff writers

The Evansville dancer and choreographer who helped put a face on AIDS in Evansville died from complications from the disease Monday.

Myreon Taylor, 43, known as an outspoken pioneer for the rights of AIDS patients in Evansville, died at ACCESS, the AIDS Care Coordination Education Support Services at 203 NW Fifth St., where he had been living since July.

"The impact he had on Evansville is what Project Quilt is trying to do nationally," said Randy Dennison, vice president of the AIDS Resource Group of Evansville. "Every number and statistic you see associated with AIDS represents a human being."

"He really made this a personal thing in Evansville. He made people realize this is something we all face and a compassionate response is in order."

Dennison remembered a poem Taylor read at an AIDS Candlelight Vigil in 1991 in which he said "I am not my

Myreon Taylor

disease. I am me."

A graduate of Central High School, Taylor worked as a dancer, teacher, choreographer, business manager and co-artistic director of the Evansville Dance Theatre for 3½ years in the mid-1980s. He had also worked with the St. Louis Ballet, Julie Mahoney Dance Co. in New York, 2 Plus 1 Dance Ensemble, and the Chicago Free Street Theatre. He was also a member of the dance faculty at the University of Louisville.

The dedication he applied to his dancing he also applied to his AIDS work. In addition to serving at the first president of the AIDS Resource Group, Taylor was on the board of the Kentuckiana People With AIDS Coalition.

Donna Dodson, executive director of the Community AIDS Action Network in Indianapolis, said Taylor also contributed tirelessly to efforts throughout the state.

"There were times he would get on the bus at 5:30 a.m. to come to Indianapolis to attend countless meetings where he gave of himself and his talents. He will be missed."

Rhonda Stien, executive director of ACCESS, said, "He fought until the very end. Even as his body declined he could hear and communicate. We couldn't give him enough pain medication to make him go to sleep.

"I think he was afraid if he went to sleep he might die and he wasn't ready," she said.

Taylor's outspoken fight against AIDS discrimination "made other people brave," Ms. Stien said.

"People are so afraid of discrimination against themselves and their families a lot of times won't even seek medical care for themselves," she said. "He gave others strength and determination."

Because Taylor was willing to go on television and have his name published people are more open, more curious and more educated today, Ms. Stien said.

Jean Allenby Weidner, founding director of the Evansville Dance Theatre, was surprised to learn of Taylor's death, and hadn't known that Taylor had AIDS.

"He was a young man I was very fond of," she said in a telephone interview from Sarasota, Fla., where she is chairman of the board for the Sarasota Ballet of Florida. "He was very outgoing and very talented."

Taylor initially was hired for a job as a dancer with the company, "but very soon he was teaching and choreographing," she said.

"He was a very loyal person." willing to work long hours in various jobs to keep the company going."

Lynne Mowrey recalls Taylor as a "natural dancer and performer."

"When he walked on stage, something turned on inside him. He was great to watch," said Ms. Mowrey, who volunteered at the Evansville Dance Theatre at the time.

"It was an inspiration for the children to see," Ms. Mowrey said.

Evansville Courier, September 16, 1992. The death of famed choreographer/dancer Myreon Taylor. *Evansville Vanderburgh Public Library.*

After several years with Evansville Dance Theater, Taylor left Evansville to pursue other career opportunities. He reappeared in 1989 and became the face of the AIDS epidemic in Evansville. He took on the role of director of the AIDS Resource Group (ARG) and told his story frequently to audiences wherever he could find them to listen. With a board of directors active in the cause, Taylor marshaled as many resources as he could for the ARG organization, moving its headquarters into the basement of the historic Beaux-Arts 1891 Old Courthouse in downtown Evansville.

In February 1991, the *Evansville Courier* ran a feature on Taylor that described in graphic detail his onset of symptoms (collapsing on a street in Idaho) and having to tell his family. The estimate of the number of people infected in Evansville was three hundred, and there were forty active cases diagnosed in southwest Indiana, thirty of them in Vanderburgh County. Taylor told readers of the paper that he thought he might have a year or so to live. At that time, death after diagnosis was one to two years. He had survived a bout with encephalitis and managed to leave a wheelchair for a cane. At forty-two, he was looking at the end of a life that should have lasted another thirty to forty years.[89]

Myreon Taylor died on September 14, 1992, at the age of forty-three.

Act Up

The AIDS epidemic quickly grew around the nation and world in the early 1990s. In Evansville, people diagnosed with AIDS were in many cases desperate for help, faced with discrimination in employment, housing, medical care and even simple things such as transportation. The AIDS Resource Group and later Matthew 25, across the river in Henderson, Kentucky, struggled to meet the needs of people in the ever-growing population of impacted city residents.

At the Someplace Else bar in downtown Evansville, an amateur drag competition was won by several men who were normally dressed in leather/motorcycle attire. On a lark and a dare, they entered an amateur drag competition wearing high blonde beehive wigs lip-synching to the 1960s song "Leader of the Pack."

Led by Ron Wilson and Reggie Green, they won the twenty-five-dollar grand prize. The pair decided they didn't need the money and donated it to the AIDS Resource Group discretionary fund. Thinking more about the situation people affected by AIDS found themselves in, the pair put out the word in the LGBTQ community that an organization similar to the Bag Ladies in Indianapolis—who dress in drag and visit bars around the city with handbags collecting money for AIDS sufferers—was just what Evansville needed.

The group was formed in late 1993, and by the spring of 1994, it had attracted nearly thirty people who put their talents to work in amateur drag shows in Evansville and the immediate tristate area. They raised money for a separate, distinct discretionary fund that someone diagnosed and living with the AIDS virus could access for immediate emergency needs, such as a utility bill or rent, for which other agencies in town lacked resources. The B-HIVES (Brotherhood for HIV Economic Support) lasted several years until some of the leaders and organizers died and interest in continuing the group faded

In 1992, Bil Browning, Jason Westmoreland and a coterie of activists organized a group under the nationwide umbrella of ACT UP (AIDS Coalition to Unleash Power). That organization had been active in trying to increase awareness of the needs of people living with AIDS in major metropolitan areas like New York, San Francisco and Houston, Texas. Westmoreland, in a September 1992 interview, said he and his group of activists were spreading the message of anti-discrimination against AIDS victims in smaller cities like Evansville. One of the first activities ACT UP undertook in Evansville was condom distribution in bars around the city, heterosexual bars included. Browning said, "With one person dying in the United States of AIDS every seven minutes and one person becoming infected with the HIV virus every minute, it's time America realized the potential of this killer."[90]

One of the more notable public protests was on the busy Morgan Avenue thoroughfare on the northeast side of the city, in front of a large Kmart store. Kmart nationally had made the decision not to sell the recent book by Magic Johnson on avoiding the AIDS virus. The nationally known basketball star had become a worldwide figure who was living with HIV. ACT UP picketed outside the large discount retailer, which forced the group to the sidewalk along the busy road, saying they were blocking parking spaces in the less than half-full one-acre lot.[91]

In 1992, ACT UP led several protests around Evansville, challenging then mayor Frank McDonald II to make AIDS a priority and to pressure legislators to fund education and prevention measures. In September 1992, there were fifty-seven AIDS cases documented in the city, and estimates were that represented about 10 percent of the total undocumented cases, including people who carried the virus and were unaware of their status.

Courier photo by **RICHARD HICKS**

Bil Browning was one of three ACT UP members protesting at the Kmart on Morgan Avenue Wednesday.

Kmart picketed by AIDS group

Three members of an AIDS awareness group picketed a Kmart store Wednesday to protest the national chain's refusal to carry Magic Johnson's book on AIDS prevention.

The group, ACT UP, claims Kmart is hindering efforts to educate people about AIDS.

Group spokesman Bil Browning was picketing with Rob Lankford and Myra Tate along the main entrance to the Morgan Avenue store. Their signs urged people to boycott Kmart.

Education needs to take place at work, in schools and on the streets, Browning said.

"People need to educate themselves because apparently the government's not going to educate us," he said.

Kmart does not carry Johnson's book, "What You Can Do to Avoid AIDS." Johnson retired from basketball after announcing he has the virus that causes AIDS.

After about 20 minutes store manager Mark Warner asked them not to picket on the sidewalk, in the fire lanes or in the parking lot where traffic could be obstructed.

"They quietly moved to the end of the parking lot," Warner said.

The decision not to carry Johnson's book was made at the corporate level, said Warner, who referred further questions to Kmart headquarters in Troy, Mich.

"There are other major retailers who don't carry it," he said.

Kmart did not return a call for comment Wednesday but earlier said the company did stock the book at Waldenbooks, which it also owns.

Evansville Press, September 10, 1992. ACT UP coordinator Bil Browning pickets outside the Evansville Kmart store on Morgan Avenue. *Evansville Vanderburgh Public Library*.

Fired

In 1993, Larry Conway was employed as a bartender at a bistro on Evansville's East Side called the Pub, a popular watering hole for businesspeople. Conway got a bad cut on his hand the evening of March 16, 1993, and went to St. Mary's Hospital emergency room for help. Nurse Donna Elder refused to treat him when he told her he was HIV positive. Finally, a physician did see him and stitched up the cut. Conway provided a physician's release to his employer, Larry Pollock, and advised him as well that he was HIV positive. Pollock fired him.[92]

Conway filed suit through the federal Equal Employment Opportunity Commission. He also sued the hospital. He sued using his name instead of John Doe. At the time, Conway said, "Evansville is a small place where restaurant workers are concerned. Everyone would have known it was me who wasn't at the Pub anymore." Before the suit could come to trial, Pollock settled for $25,000 out of court. Later, Conway worked as a clerical employee for ARG. In the settlement, Pollock agreed to begin AIDS sensitivity training for employees at his establishment. Conway passed away on June 24, 1998, at his home. He had spoken many times statewide for the National Association of People with AIDS organization.[93] In keeping with the deep thread of irony that runs through Evansville's history, the Pub later became a gay bar called Scandals, operated from 2015 to about 2018 by Aaron Hurley and Michael Stoker (Lady Jasmine).

AIDS Resource Group

As AIDS moved through the Evansville population, several notable events occurred that have continued to the present. In 1990, the board of the ARG partnered with an urban Catholic ministry at the St. Mary's Church in downtown Evansville to host the first of many annual candlelight services memorializing AIDS victims. For several years, the services drew large crowds who contributed money to the ARG discretionary fund that provided direct client assistance. The church eventually changed its leadership and eliminated any LGBTQ programming within it. The more affirming First Presbyterian Church on Southeast Second Street became more a focal point for LGBTQ-themed events.

In 1991, a major motion picture company came to Evansville to film *A League of Their Own*, a comedy about the 1940s-era women's baseball league. A portion of the movie was filmed at the historic Bosse Field baseball stadium. One of the stars of the film who stayed in Evansville for a short time was singer Madonna. The celebrity actress made few friends while in Evansville, and her commentary later about the river city was anything but positive. She visited one of the local gay bars once, Sho Bar, and famously signed the wall but again made few friends there.

In January 1992, ARG announced that, in addition to a $2,500 outright gift, Madonna had paid for a full-page ad in the arts and entertainment national *Billboard* magazine listing the Evansville AIDS organization as one of the HIV charities she supported and encouraged others to do so. The ad and a supplemental *USA Today* story about it led to several phone inquiries from other cities and some donations.

The arts community took on an awareness campaign and fundraising as well. In May 1992, a wealthy Posey County man named Jerry Wade, who was living in New York, sold his New Harmony, Indiana home that contained an art collection with an estimated $10,000 value. The collection had works from a variety of local artists that Wade had acquired at auctions over a period of years. Working with a New Harmony gallery, Wade agreed to offer the entire collection at an auction that drew over one hundred art collectors. In addition, several New Harmony and Evansville antique and collectable shops donated pieces of silver, glassware and other valuables to be included. A pastel work by artist and USI Art professor Katie Waters became the focal point of a hotly contested bidding war, the most active of the event, and sold for $1,000, a high price at the time for local artwork, even by someone with a national reputation. The overarching message of the event was that AIDS was finally out of the closet and it was safe for community leaders to support the effort to help people with the disease.

What started happening in the early 1990s changed the outlook on ARG for a decade. Young men, many of whom left Evansville after college, were either dying in other cities or returning home to die with family. These young men were in their thirties generally and had for the most part grown up in Evansville. In some cases, the family would put a notation at the end of the obituary that memorial contributions could be made to ARG, one way of saying how that person had died.

The AIDS Walk, created by ARG board member and TV personality April Mitchell in 1993 in memory of her brother who died, grew exponentially in the 1990s. From a humble beginning at the campus of the University of Southern Indiana on the far west side in 1994, the walk started at the Old Courthouse and wound its way around the entire downtown. Hundreds participated, including numerous high school clubs and college fraternities and sororities, which had worked to raise money at school events for the walk. The 1994 walk was so successful it raised over $16,000, or 10 percent of the organization's entire budget.[94]

ANDY WRIGHT (1950–1994): TURNING GRIEF INTO WORK

Andy Wright and sister Ann Wright Tornatta, circa 1985. *Ann Tornatta.*

One of the most tragic losses to an Evansville family came in 1994, when Andy Wright, son of a Cadillac dealership family, died in New York City. The alumnus of Evansville's Harrison High School and Washington University in St. Louis was a luminous figure in the world of television. A 1980 *Evansville Press* article described the young man in glowing terms as the head of Ted Turner's new WTBS cable network's art department. He had worked for both CBS and NBC television networks in graphic design and was a principal designer for the then-new CNN. Wright won an Emmy in April 1978 for his work in news graphics. A futurist, he predicted in the 1980 article, "People will have memory banks on their TV which will be able to record programming distributed to the home."[95]

Wright died of AIDS in July 1994 at the age of forty-three. His sister, Ann Wright Tornatta (then Ann Wright Steagall), joined the board of ARG, determined to help the agency raise money for other people suffering this tragic fate. Ann says today looking back on her brother's life, "He was so forward thinking. I miss him so much. He was my best friend." Wright would have been seventy-two years old today.

SAM RYAN: TURNING GRIEF INTO A MIRACLE

Another important Evansville event in the history of the effort to support AIDS victims occurred in the spring of 1995. Sam Ryan was the son of George and Martha Ryan, a wealthy and socially prominent Evansville couple. A drug and alcohol counselor, Ryan had moved to Florida, where he died of AIDS at thirty-three on February 2, 1995. The devastated parents were good friends with the director of the Evansville Museum, John Streetman. Streetman, in addition to being a museum official, was a songwriter/composer known in various art circles and had written a significant portfolio of music. Streetman joined the ARG board in 1995

Above: The 1996 cover of *Songs for Life* with composer John Streetman, a spectacular fundraiser for the AIDS Resource Group. This helped change the community's attitude about HIV/AIDS. *John Streetman*.

Left: Sam Ryan (1960–1993), in whose memory the *Songs for Life* album was produced by his parents, George and Martha Ryan. Sam was beloved by friends in Evansville. *John Streetman*.

after Ryan's passing and, together with his parents, decided to produce a major fundraising item for ARG: a professionally produced compact disc album of his favorite self-composed songs. The album would be called *Songs for Friends and Lovers*. The Ryans said their son loved music, and it seemed a fitting way to memorialize him.

On April 22, 1996, in the elegant Old Gallery at the Evansville Museum at 6:30 p.m., more than two hundred of the city's wealthy and prominent people gathered at a premiere party featuring local cabaret singer Cary Gray; Broadway singer Tim Ewing, a native of the city; and Bill McKinley, another well-known recording artist from Indianapolis who had appeared with Gray in several stage shows over the years. They performed selections from the album.[96] The musicians, who had gathered in a New York studio to record the album, came to Evansville for the premiere party.

The Ryans had returned from their Naples, Florida home for the event and were tearfully overjoyed that this gift they had underwritten in their beloved son's name was a reality. Lines were long as ARG staff and board members sold the CDs as fast as they could.

At a debriefing for the ARG team the following week, Streetman expressed his thanks for the organized chaos that had made the album such a success. It was nominated for several Grammys the following year.

As drug cocktails and treatments improved, people began living with HIV much longer. Today, there are people in Evansville who have lived with HIV for more than thirty years and are in their sixties—a testimony to science and the care that ARG provided to help them live better, longer lives. Stacey Easley, the current director of ARG, reported that in Evansville, they tracked 158 persons who died in the years ARG has served.

A partner agency in Henderson, Kentucky, Matthew 25 is an expansive clinic facility that began life in 1996 as a few volunteers and has grown into a more than sixty-staff agency that provides various services to the HIV-positive community and provides testing and new PREP treatments. Matthew 25 has counted 162 deaths among its clientele and currently serves more than 700 patients in the area.[97]

CHAPTER II

BEGINNINGS OF ORGANIZED QUEER LIFE INTO THE MODERN ERA

Paul, a seventy-nine-year-old retired man who has lived in Evansville most of his life, was instrumental in attempting the first efforts at organized queer life in the city. There were no official places gay and lesbian people could congregate without raising alarms. Paul said that he and a small group of other like-minded men wanted to entertain other gay people as female impersonators. They had done several shows for fun in people's homes and in country cabins by invitation, but they longed for "more legitimate" venues because disgruntled non-invitees almost always had the private events raided by alcohol enforcement officials.

Paul went to the owners of the bar in the Vendome Hotel at Third and Sycamore Streets in late 1959 and offered to perform drag shows on certain nights for tips only. He promised crowds of gay people would help build business in the bar. The Vendome did not have a good reputation at this time because newer hotels in the city were attracting the business traveler, and the bar was languishing. The owners agreed, and on certain nights, Paul became the Dazzling Denise Nichols. His troupe performed, lip-synching to the standards of the day. It took some time for word to spread around town, but after about five months, crowds began coming to the Empire Room to see the drag shows and mix and mingle.

Paul said law enforcement was a constant battle, as was the Alcohol and Beverage Commission (ABC). Paul said one ABC officer in particular was a problem because he knew his oldest son was a homosexual who frequented the shows. Paul said the drag performers would sometimes hide the young man in a mop closet to keep his father from finding him in their raids.

Above: Vendome Hotel, demolished in 1972, was the site of the first organized drag revue in Evansville, circa 1960s. *Evansville Vanderburgh Public Library*.

Opposite: The Dazzling Denise Nichols at the Vendome Hotel drag show, circa 1963. *Denise Nichols*.

The bar at the Vendome didn't last long because the owners decided after a few years that the risk wasn't worth the small profits. In 1964, Denise and her drag troupe found themselves without a venue, and organized queer life stopped again. But that didn't last long.

At the intersection of Fulton Avenue and Pennsylvania, a supper club was built in 1954. Nell and Eddie Ward opened Ward's Steak House that July. The Wards sold the business to Jack Brown and James Moers, who renamed it the Pal's Steak House in 1956. They sold it to Edgar and Edna Painter in 1958. The Painters at one time owned the Cameron Mansion, built in 1943 for Hollywood actress June Knight Cameron. They eventually sold the business to Pete Mosby, who became dissatisfied with the capacity of

the place. Because of Evansville's repressive attitude about sex, Mosby was brought up on charges of selling condoms in a machine in the men's room. On September 21, 1961, Judge Claude Bates threw out the case, saying the bar owner wasn't selling the condoms; the machine company was. Mosby sold the business to Joe and Joan Kluemper, who also bought the rights to the name. Mosby built his new Pete's Supper Club several blocks west.

The Kluempers, a couple who had been frequent audience members at the Vendome shows and now owned their own club, invited Paul and his troupe of queens to perform at their new venue. The drag shows opened on the Fourth of July 1968, headlined by the Dazzling Denise Nichols.

The Pal's became the first real center of queer life in Evansville. Patrons mostly entered the establishment by the door facing south, which did not exit out to traffic on Division Street. It was not far from the Union Depot, where the Louisville and Nashville Railroad still provided passenger rail service. The Pal's became a focal point for both queer audiences and local gossip. Occasionally, heterosexual couples came to the club to see the shows and also see if they recognized LGBTQ people there as patrons.

Violence was never far away. Bruce Sailer, then twenty-six, was nearly beaten to death in the parking lot of the Pal on the night of June 26, 1971. Police found him lying on a ramp at the nearby Orr Iron building and arrested him for public intoxication, even though he was bloody and nearly unconscious. He told the officers he'd been beaten, but they arrested him and did not seek medical attention for him. In the article about the incident, the newspaper identified him as a "beautician from Mt. Vernon." His brother hurriedly bailed him out and rushed him to Welborn Hospital, where he was admitted in critical condition. There is no record of a lawsuit, but the brother demanded an investigation about why Sailer sat in the jail for seven hours lapsing in and out of consciousness.[98]

Pal's had a brush with celebrity one evening. Film and stage star Leslie Uggams, who was appearing in the showroom lounge at the Executive Inn, heard about the drag revue at the Pal's and came to the bar after

Everything NEW EXCEPT The Management

Ward's Steak House

FULTON AVENUE at PENNSYLVANIA STS.

FOR RESERVATIONS—PHONE 2-0863

LARGE DINING ROOM
•
PRIVATE DINING ROOM
•
COMPLETE BAR SERVICE
•
CHECK ROOM
•
ENTIRE BUILDING AIR CONDITIONED
•
LARGE PARKING LOT IN REAR

Here's what Evansville has been waiting for / A brand new, modern place to eat . . . with every convenience . . . at a price ANYONE can afford. Inside and out Nell and Eddie Ward's place . . . offers you and your family the best for less.

Featuring JACK BROWN At The PIANO And ORGAN Every Evening

8 P.M. TILL 12 P.M.

NOON LUNCHES and TYPICAL MENU

Choice of—
Meat
Vegetables
Salad
Bread & Butter ..... 65¢

Roast Beef & Gravy
Mashed Potatoes
Peas or Corn
Combination Salad
Bread & Butter ...... 65¢

WARD'S SPECIAL

½ Spring Chicken, Combination Salad, French Fries, Hot Rolls and Butter $1.50

STEAKS

12-Oz. Club Steak $2.00
16-Oz. T-Bone Steak $2.75
Filet Mignon Steak $3.00

Includes French Fried Potatoes, Salad, Hot Rolls & Butter.

WE RECOMMEND

Our Own Fresh Vegetable Soup 20c
A Hamburger, Wimpy would love 25c
Home-made Chili with Oyster Crackers 25c
Italian Spaghetti with Meat Sauce 85c

OPEN EVERY DAY EXCEPT SUNDAY

• NOON LUNCHES 11 A.M. to 2 P.M.
• FOOD SERVED 11 A.M. to 11:30 P.M.
• BAR OPEN 10 A.M. to 12 P.M.

We Thank the Following Concerns Who Helped Make Our Opening Possible:

BRUCKEN COMPANY, INC.
Store & Restaurant Fixtures
122 N. W. First St., Ph. 3-4416

Carrier Air Conditioning By . . .
GEORGE KOCH SONS, INC.
Evansville, Ind.

Holland
CUSTARD & ICE CREAM INC
The Growing Name In Dairy Products

WARWEG & HAGEL
Architects
306 Grein Building

AMUSEMENT CORPORATION
322 N. W. 6th St. Ph. 5-9887

Compliments of
Sunbeam
The Right Energy Bread

BLUE BIRD PIE CO., Inc.
Be Wise . . . Use Blue Bird Pies

GRIESE WALL & FLOOR COVERING COMPANY
809 N. Main St. Ph. 4-5988

SWANSON-NUNN SIGNS, INC.
2018 S. Kentucky Ave. Ph. 4-5596

LOEHRLEIN BROS. CONSTRUCTION AND SUPPLY CO.
407 E. Columbia. Ph. 5-1162

WOLFLIN WEST SIDE LUMBER CO.
421 N. St. Joseph Ave. Ph. 5-7108

STAHL PACKING CO.
"Better Brand" Meats
6th & Ingle Sts. Ph. 2-1126

CRAIG POULTRY CO.
Lincoln at Governor. Ph. 5-8259

Hesmer's
FINE FOODS
BETTER because they are FRESH

Above: Ward's Steak House at the corner of Fulton and Division. Built in 1954, in 1968 it became the Pal's Steak House and Evansville's first true gay bar where LGBTQ people could have community and socialization. It was demolished in the 1980s with the Lloyd Expressway construction. *Evansville Vanderburgh Public Library*.

Opposite: An ashtray depicting the logo for the Pal's Steakhouse, the first openly LGBTQ gathering spot in Evansville, circa 1970. A rare memento. *Rachael Evans*.

her show. She had, so it is told, such a good time that she joined the queens on stage and sang a song with them. There is no documentation to prove this story, but it does seem likely. In later years, some Hollywood celebrities visiting the city would locate a gay club to visit, knowing they'd be welcomed by a more diverse crowd.

A male couple named Duke and Kenny opened a bar called the Hawaiian Village at the corner of Third Street and Sycamore across from the Greyhound bus station. It had earlier been the Manhattan Bar. From 1966 until it closed in 1968 after losing its liquor license (Duke served a nineteen-year-old visiting basketball player a drink), gay men in their twenties flocked to the Pacific-themed bar. The Alcohol Beverage Commission gave its reason for not renewing the license as "failure to maintain an acceptable reputation."[99]

There were several bars in the mid-1970s that welcomed a gay clientele, although they were smaller neighborhood establishments, much like on the TV show *Cheers*, where everyone knew your name. People who frequented the Cabaret, for instance, were mainly women, although men were present in smaller numbers. The Cabaret, located at 1331 South Elliot Street on the south side of the city in a mainly residential area, usually saw motorcycles parked nearby, as many of the women who partied there were riders.

Earlier in the 1970s, what had been known as the Silver Saddle and then Tony's Bar became, for a short time, a gay bar called the Happy Hour. There were limited drag shows, as the stage was small, but it could become crowded late. The new owners renamed it the Cabaret. Older men remember it mainly as a women's bar (the owners were a lesbian couple) but said that they never felt unwelcome. The bar was the scene of the shooting of a young man in the parking lot in September 1978 by someone in a passing car. Most of the patrons suspected it was a hate crime. The Cabaret was later purchased by Robert Neil Campbell and his wife, Ellen, and reopened as Campbell's, which featured a DJ and dancing but also a ping-pong table.[100]

During the early 1970s, a small bar named Ramond's was open to LGBTQ patrons, though it was not advertised as such. An Evansville police vice squad officer, Charles Wiley, testified before the Alcohol Beverage Commission that Ramond's is "frequented by homosexuals which is not good for the high and fine reputation a tavern is supposed to have to maintain such a liquor license." Jacob Acker, the bar manager, objected to Wiley's comments and retorted, "It's a free country; no one has the right to discriminate as to who can come in and have a beer." Ramond's was not open very long, having been raided several times for underage drinking and other complaints.[101]

There was a small bar opened near the former location of the Pal, called My Way, in a former small restaurant at what was Fulton and High Street before High was eliminated. The My Way was open only about a year before it was converted into an "adult emporium" and a strip club called Scores.

In the early spring of 1979, a group of gay men approached Jim and Norma Black, owners of a strip club located on West Maryland Street at the corner of Eleventh Avenue, about transforming their failing tavern called the Swinging Door into a gay bar. In 1977, the Indiana legislature finally passed a repeal of the 1881 sodomy law, and as in many other states, LGBTQ people were finally liberated from the threat of incarceration for their sexual identity. Such bars and clubs were blossoming around the nation. The *Evansville Courier* ran several stories about the increasing openness of gay communities and the political clout they were accumulating. Norma Black was the driving force behind the conversion of the bar and allowed Michael Wilson and a small coterie of friends to transform the interior into a dance club complete with rotating disco lights, a mirrored dance floor and an expanded DJ booth.

Tori Daniels, Miss Gay Evansville 1983, performs her winning song, "Le Jazz Hot," from the film *Victor/Victoria*. *Rachael Malone.*

In April 1979, the Evansville newspapers ran for the first time an advertisement for an "alternative nightclub" complete with the scientific symbols for men and women together as same-sex pairings, which let everyone know what kind of place it was going to be. From the moment the bar opened on April 26, 1979, LGBTQ people—though mostly cisgendered men at first—packed the place. For a while, people just called it the Door and, when with strangers, simply called it "the bar."[102]

Wilson belonged to a DJ pool out of Nashville, Tennessee, and would receive several copies of the newest club 12-inch, 33-rpm disco singles each month. He would present the copies as gifts to friends with little stickers noting who it was for, the date and an occasion if there was one, such as a birthday. While the mainstream dance clubs in Evansville like Funky's and Good Time Bobby's played current mainstream dance music, the smart young heterosexuals who loved to dance knew to hit the gay bar after midnight to get the latest and hottest dance music fresh from the coasts.

The drag entertainers, both male and female impersonators, found a home at last. Several who had performed at the Pal's took their places at the Swinging Door. Lori Reynolds, Jeanette Wylde, Bella Donna, Samantha and Wanda Walker (called Wicked Wanda) were already familiar names in drag culture. By the early 1980s, drag entertainment was beginning to take on more of a professional look in Evansville, although amateurs were welcome to try out their art as well on "off nights."

In those early 1980s, antigay violence was becoming more frequent. Young men in the city would harass, threaten and many times assault lone gay people they found walking to a car or walking toward the bar. Jim Black hired an off-duty police officer as security on Friday and Saturday nights, which helped quell some of the violence. In response to this uptick in street violence, Yvon Mabrey and her partner laid the groundwork for an advocacy group to provide an additional organization for LGBTQ persons in Evansville and the surrounding area called the Tri State Alliance (TSA) for Gays and Lesbians. It was incorporated in 1983 and met in the Universal Unitarian Fellowship Church, a liberal nondenominational group that at the time was one of the few religious orders that welcomed gay people openly.[103]

The group was small and for years did not dare print its leadership or members' names for fear of retaliation from employers or family who did not know their sexual identity. TSA published the first focused newsletter, which was mailed in a plain envelope without identifying its origin, to a private mailing list. The newsletter let readers know what was happening in their community and the world at large, civil rights cases going on in the United States and what businesses were gay-friendly at the time. The newsletter was a window into an otherwise invisible world. For all its secrecy and difficulty, it was the beginning of an existence that some in Evansville had hoped would stay closed forever. The early days of the Tri State Alliance did feature some public events. Early picnics at Wesselman's Park on the East Side attracted some younger LGBTQ people, and there was a bowling

'Sick' threats denounced by member of gay group

By RON SYNOVITZ
Courier staff writer

Anti-gay fliers recently posted along Southeast First Street demonstrate why only about 5 percent of Evansville's homosexual community is "out-of-the-closet," a spokesman for a local gay support group said Friday.

Many Tri-State gays fear they will lose their jobs, or in some cases, even become victims of violent "homophobics" if they publicly announce their sexual preference, said a gay member of Tri-State Alliance. The man asked that his name not be published for those reasons.

Sometime late Thursday or early Friday, an unknown person posted more than a dozen placards along the 300 and 400 blocks of Southeast First Street declaring "open hunting season" on gays.

Decorated with illustrations of handguns, one sign said "Go ahead, homos, make my 357." Another warned, "This area is protected from Faggots." By Friday afternoon, most of the signs had been torn down. More were posted Friday night.

"I think someone is pretty sick," said the Tri-State Alliance spokesman. "If there is a problem in that neighborhood, I believe it is by a very small percent-

See THREATS on Page 3

This anti-gay sign was posted along Southeast First Street. Courier photo by RICHARD HICKS

Evansville Press, May 13, 1983, shows signs posted in historic area where gay men cruised. The threat of violence led to the start of the Tri State Alliance. *Evansville Vanderburgh Public Library*.

league that attracted some negative attention at one of the bowling alleys in the city. However, the participants had fun and enjoyed some community with one another. Those early pioneers should be credited with starting great changes that were to come.

THE 1980s

Queer life took on an identity of its own as the 1980s progressed. A second bar opened on Morgan Avenue in 1984. The former Johnny K's country western bar on the far northeast side opened as the Other Side II. It would later become Club East. The newest bar was much larger than the Swinging Door and had a separate showroom from the main dance bar. Although the disco era had begun to pass away after 1980, dance music was still a major draw for the young set in Evansville. Bars were the places LGBTQ people felt safe and accepted in those days.

The Other Side showroom was the place to be on Saturday night as the drag culture was coming into its own, after having restarted at the Swinging Door. That two gay bars could operate in Evansville was considered incredible for the time, but the Swinging Door did not survive the decade, closing in 1987. The Other Side II was frequently the target of the ABC just as the older bars had been. Underage patrons were occasionally found, and the bar owner got in trouble. But the club carried on despite several small fires over the years, one caused by drag performer Jeanette Wylde, who, in preparation for a tropical number, lit tiki torches on stage, setting some ceiling tiles on fire.[104]

Another bar that converted to a gay clientele was the Mecca Bar at 700 Division Street, just west of Kentucky Avenue. Renamed the My Way Bar, it opened as a gay club in September 1981 but was destroyed by an arson fire in January 1982. The owners of the bar, David Rager and his wife, Margaret, were heterosexuals who wanted to open and operate a club for LGBTQ people.

The day after the blaze, Margaret told newspapers that she had heard about threats to burn down the business because it welcomed gay people and some in the city were opposed. For forty years, the old Mecca Bar had been a drawing card for Evansville people in the downtown area, and in the 1950s, it was raided for gambling and other vice.

The Ragers had remodeled the bar, adding a bigger dance floor and stage area. Four drag performers lived in the apartment above the bar but were in Memphis the night of the fire, January 25, 1982. In 1983, Rager was arrested and charged with burning down his own business, and a forty-two-year-old man, Danny Decker, accused him of paying $1,000 for the arson. Decker admitted he set the blaze but said that he was paid to. Decker was convicted at trial on January 31, 1983. His sentence of five years was reduced to two years because he testified against Rager and turned in evidence in other crimes as well. When Rager's trial occurred in January 1984, after listening to all the testimony, Judge Randall Shepard, later chief justice of the Indiana Supreme Court, ruled in a directed verdict that Rager was innocent. There was much inconsistency in Decker's testimony, which led to doubt about Rager's involvement.[105]

The 1990s

In an industrial and high-poverty area on East Franklin Street, the Sho Bar, an older neighborhood bar and then a strip club, turned into a gay bar around the turn of the decade and for a time was the most popular gay nightspot. During the Evansville time of filming the 1991 movie *A League of Their Own*, a film about a World War II–era girls' baseball league, the popular stars of the film staying in Evansville made celebrated visits to the Sho Bar. Madonna, the gay icon, famously signed the wall in the main bar room. She didn't mingle with bar patrons, however, and later made disparaging remarks about the city, which drew some criticism. The filming of a Hollywood movie in Evansville occupied the summer media and gossip around town. Other celebrities seen at the gay club were Tom Hanks and director Penny Marshall, who were a bit friendlier to locals. The Sho Bar suddenly became the talk of the town. Its location was not ideal, and after Someplace Else opened downtown, the Sho Bar became a college bar and eventually was destroyed by fire.

On February 7, 1992, the *Evansville Courier* business page announced a new gay bar, Teena Faye's, had opened in the former Amanda Fenwick's restaurant on the riverfront at Main and Riverside. The building was constructed in 1976 to resemble an old-style paddlewheel riverboat. Over a fifteen-year period, various occupants opened and closed, unable to make a success of the business. Once Teena Faye opened her nightclub, many Saturday nights there were lines of people waiting to get inside. The dance floor in the center of the main room, surrounded by booths that remained from its restaurant days, also served as the drag stage. The *Evansville Courier* article announcing its opening was the first time the words "gay bar" were used to describe an Evansville business. It stated that the bar would be owned by Pat and Shirley Winchell who also owned a country western bar called Chances R and a strip club on North Main called the Playgirl. The Winchells said Teena Faye would manage the new bar and it would be named for her, as she "had been around the gay community for years." They felt that there needed to be a quality, safe place for gays to socialize.[106]

Teena Faye's survived for several years, even as the Frank McDonald II administration pushed hard for downtown redevelopment and closure of the gay bar on the riverfront. Rumors in the LGBTQ community were that McDonald thought having a gay establishment on the riverfront was a detriment to the reputation of the area. There is no evidence that he felt that way, however. The location is now the eight-story Old National Bank.

Another bar opened on the southside along South Kentucky Avenue, at one time U.S. 41. A restaurant called Andy's Steak and Barrel became Scottie's. The late Bill Bell, an icon in queer Evansville history, opened the nightclub on December 4, 1997. It featured at one time a piano bar, an expansive plant-filled patio and a showroom for drag revues. Scottie's mainly attracted a more mature clientele, but younger people would come as well, depending on the crowd level at other places. Scottie's had a more relaxed atmosphere. Bell closed the bar after several years and passed away after suffering long illnesses for several years. He was a funny, energetic man who owned several other businesses in the community and offered jobs to many younger people who couldn't find work elsewhere.

In 1990, Ellen Campbell, who had owned Campbell's, purchased a restaurant/bar on the edge of the northeastern section of downtown, on the part of Main Street disconnected from the main business district when the Civic Center government complex was built, cutting Main in half. She reopened Someplace Else, which for years had been a gathering spot for Republican politicians and their supporters, where business deals were made and community leaders drank toasts to one another. When Ellen decided to change her bar into an "alternative" establishment in 1993, the draw of the new bar precipitated the closing of Teena Faye's and the eventual demolition of the building.

Someplace Else continues to operate, although Ellen Campbell died in 2010. She was "mother hen" to hundreds of queer people in the years she owned and operated her bar. She knew nearly everyone by name who came in and kept an eye out for potential troublemakers. She was the caretaker for a generation of gay men and women who returned her affection many times over. In an early attempt at hosting a Pride celebration, Someplace Else would get a street closure from the city administration and host a street party in the summer, inviting celebrities to appear on stage along with local drag performers. Disco superstar Maxine Nightingale was a guest artist, as was Coco Peru, a drag star noted for her appearances in film and television. The street festivals lasted a few years but ended in 2008.

With Ellen's death, her granddaughter Belinda Breivogel inherited the bar and decided to retain its LGBTQ definition and has carried on the name of the bar until today. It is one of the oldest continuously operating gay bars in the Midwest.

Andrew Sneed

One of the last murders of an LGBTQ cis man where the accused used sexual advances as an excuse for murder occurred in August 2000. Andrew Jeffrey Sneed befriended a man named Willian Hornbostel at Someplace Else. Technically homeless, Hornbostel couldn't go to the men's shelter due to his intoxication. Sneed invited him to sleep at his apartment at 800 SE Second street at about 3:00 a.m. on the early morning of August 26.

The following Sunday, Hornbostel was at a gas station on North Fares Avenue with Sneed's car. In the back were several pieces of Sneed's electronics. A woman reported she bought a VCR from him at the station. Hornbostel bought gas and drove to Kentucky, where he was involved in a car accident. He told arresting officers who tested him for drunken driving that he had borrowed the car from a friend in Evansville. Police tried to call

Sneed, but there was no answer. They called Sneed's parents, who called Evansville police, who found his dead body folded up partially in a sofa bed. He had been strangled to death. In fact, the autopsy showed his larynx and bones in his throat had been crushed, as if someone stomped on them with a boot or shoe.

At trial, prosecutor Stan Levco noted for the jury that Hornbostel was more concerned with the public thinking he was gay than with being a murderer. In fact, his defense counsel did make the statement that Hornbostel was not a homosexual but that he had gone to Someplace Else to drink because he knew it was open until 3:00 a.m. Hornbostel said he was awakened by Sneed's sexual advances three times as he tried to sleep, and in the "heat of the moment," he choked Sneed to "get him off of me." He said the level of "crank" in his system was such that he didn't realize Sneed was dead until it was too late.

Hornbostel was convicted of murder and of being a habitual criminal in December 2000 and received a sentence of ninety-six years. The *Courier and Press* article noted that the death of the Sneeds' son was very painful for the family, especially his father. "He loved his son," his mother was quoted as saying. "Andy was a very outgoing person and loved animals and gardening." The conviction was upheld by the Indiana Court of Appeals on October 19, 2001.[107]

Evansville witnessed violence against transgender people in July 2016. A transwoman, Crystal Cash, fifty-five, who lived and worked in an apartment building in the 700 block of North First Avenue, was shot in the head by twenty-seven-year-old Gerald Lewis. Cash said he asked to use her bathroom, having encountered her on the sidewalk. She reported to police that he shouted a homophobic slur as he fired. Cash also reported that police responding refused to use her chosen pronouns or name, which led to some voluntary sensitivity training within the law enforcement team. Lewis was judged incompetent to stand trial and was confined to a mental facility.

Digging into Cash's background and business, the local daily paper insinuated she was a sex worker and mentioned in several articles websites she used to advertise her businesses. Cash considered it media victim-blaming for violence perpetrated against her, a situation that happens to many transwomen in America.[108]

Pride

After some controversies became public involving the Tri State Alliance in 2018, a group of LGBTQ people and several heterosexual allies formed a new nonprofit organization called River City Pride, which expanded the vision of the local gay community and instituted a Pride celebration to replicate those that had long since taken place in larger cities. In June 2019, the organizers and the founder, Emil Lamar, were surprised at the turnout of non-LGBTQ citizens who watched the hourlong parade through the downtown and came to the festival featuring a drag show and vendors at Haynie's Corner. The estimated attendance at both events that June Saturday were upward of five thousand, something that would have been impossible just a few years earlier. The Pride celebrations were interrupted by the COVID-19 pandemic in 2020 and 2021, but in 2021, a new organization, Hudson and Reed (named for gay actors Rock Hudson and Robert Reed by a young Hollywood history devotee named James Kemmerer), offered a socially distanced Pride in the Park event featuring arts and craft vendors and an evening drag show. A crowd of five hundred or so turned out for the evening in the city's urban Garvin Park. River City Pride returned with its parade and festival in 2022 and drew similar large crowds for both. Unlike other smaller cities where Pride events were protested by local political and religious entities, Evansville's were not under attack.

In the modern political era in Evansville, one of the earliest supporters of LGBTQ rights was State Representative Dennis Avery, who represented the western section of Evansville extending into Posey County. He was the first political officeholder to meet with a gay audience when the early Tri State Alliance invited several officeholders to meet with the organization and discuss state and local issues.

Another very vocal supporter of LBGTQ rights was the Reverend Phil Hoy, who was elected to the Vanderburgh County Council and later to the District 77 Indiana House seat from this area. Hoy faced blistering criticism from a right-wing Republican opponent, David Hennig, in the 2004 election when Hennig ran radio and TV advertisements accusing Hoy of performing "homosexual weddings" and trying to legally marry gay people when it was not legal.[109]

Hoy defended his ministry at the Zion United Church of Christ in Henderson, Kentucky, as "open and affirming" and did not deny that he performed "commitment ceremonies" for same-sex couples. He refused to debate the issue with Hennig, who also hit him for being pro-choice on abortion rights. Hoy won the election as a Democrat in a year that saw sweeping Republican victories. At the time, Hoy declared marriage was between "one man and one woman" but opposed the GOP-supported Indiana Constitutional Amendment, which would have codified that opinion. Hoy later changed his public opinion on marriage and supported full marriage rights for same-sex couples.[110]

Hoy faced the same attack ads in 2006 from another Republican opponent, Andrew Smith. This time, Republican party leaders agreed to state publicly that they did not favor discrimination or inflammatory statements against LGBTQ people.

During the 2006 election season, one of the largest private fundraising events occurred at the East Side home of a gay couple and attracted many community members to support the congressional candidacy of then-sheriff Brad Ellsworth, who ended up winning the seat in a landslide over the incumbent anti-gay John Hostettler. Also attending that fundraiser were Hoy, sheriff candidate Eric Williams and State Representative Dennis Avery, among others.

In 2011, during his first campaign for mayor (his first of three terms), then–county commissioner Lloyd Winnecke was asked by a student in an appearance at Central High School what he considered his most significant difference from his national Republican Party brethren. Without hesitation, he said it was the attitude about gay rights in America. As noted earlier, it was his sister, Joycelyn, who wrote the expansive *Sunday Courier and Press* article surveying LGBTQ lives in 1981.

For several years, the Evansville City Council has approved a resolution (8–1) marking Pride Month. Councilman Justin Elpers, the hyper-conservative councilman, has always been the "nay" vote for that non-binding resolution. Interestingly, Elpers, in his 2015 campaign, appeared at a Tri State Alliance candidates forum where he pledged to support adding "teeth" to the human relations ordinance regarding sexual orientation and gender identity. As an elected councilman, he voted against it. Elpers has been an unceasing critic of the LGBTQ community. He spends his time discussing photographs of males in drag to audiences and was an outspoken critic of the public library's Drag Queen Story Hour, which is discussed later. He follows a pattern of male Republican politicians who focus much energy on gay issues. Interestingly, in 2018, he participated in an LGBTQ-sponsored all-male fashion revue and comedic "beauty contest."

CHAPTER 12

DRAG AND THE CURRENT CLIMATE IN THE RIVER CITY

Any discussion about Evansville and its LGBTQ history must address drag. The term itself, according to the Webster dictionary, dates back to the 1880s, when men, dressed as women in stage performances, wore dresses so long that they "dragged" the floor. It became a term synonymous with wearing apparel opposite to one's gender or regular identity. For centuries, women were not permitted to take part in stage productions/theater, so men played all roles, including female ones. In England during the Elizabethan period, women weren't permitted to take part until 1660.

However, the art of female impersonation wasn't widespread (other than for humor) until the period in American entertainment we know as vaudeville. In the late nineteenth and early twentieth centuries, during which silent films became a universal form of mass entertainment, theaters featured live productions with a variety of acts that many times included singers, actors, jugglers, acrobats and other performers before live audiences. Later, those acts accompanied one- or two-reel silent movies.

In Evansville, the premier houses for vaudeville were the New Grand Theater, which stood on Sycamore Street between Second and Third Streets, and the Well's Bijou, which stood on Third Street near Locust. They were enormous houses, with several rows of balcony seats and a large stage. Later, movie screens were installed that rolled down for showing films in each. The Bijou burned down in 1923, but the Grand lasted until 1962. Evansville theaters were on the national circuit for top-rated vaudeville and Broadway touring companies.

Several times over the course of the second decade of the twentieth century, Evansville welcomed performances by the most famous female impersonator of the day, Julian Eltinge, who made a career out of playing female roles and the illusion of being a woman. Eltinge was known internationally and quite celebrated for his talent.

In 1916, the *Evansville Courier* heavily promoted his appearance at the Well's Bijou in a production of *Cousin Lucy* in which he portrayed both a male and a female. Photos of Eltinge in full drag were published in the newspapers, and a glowing preview of the performance was published on March 20, 1916:

> *The soul of the feminine sex promises to be stirred to a state of ecstasy during the dress making scene which forms the second part of the piece. It is said that nothing quite so dazzling in its luxuriousness has ever before been put on the stage. It is in this act that Eltinge himself acts as model to show off gown after gown to prospective fashion buyers. All of the frocks, wraps and hats worn by Julian Eltinge in this and the other scenes of "Cousin Lucy" are furnished by the foremost dressmaking house in New York and represent the forthcoming modes of feminine apparel.*[111]

In July 1977, the Executive Inn showroom lounge featured a drag performer named Jim Bailey, who had made a national name for himself on TV by impersonating such celebrities as Judy Garland and Barbra Streisand, using makeup, wigs and his own singing voice, with which he could remarkably mimic several famous female singers. All of Bailey's shows were sold out, and the reviews in the daily newspapers were positive.

The July 11, 1977 *Evansville Courier* put it this way:

> *No impersonator, Bailey calls himself an illusionist. And his illusions are so compelling, so true to life that the audience becomes so immersed in his character they forget he is not the real Judy Garland, Peggy Lee or Barbra Streisand he is creating for them. When he "did" Barbra on the* Carol Burnette Show, *the real Streisand was watching and reportedly sent Burnette a letter asking where her check was. Judy was delighted with his rendition of her, and Judy's daughters, Liza Minelli and Lorna Luft, are two of his biggest fans.*[112]

There was no protest or controversy in any of the appearances of Eltinge in Evansville; in fact, all of his performances sold out. Some would argue

Amusements

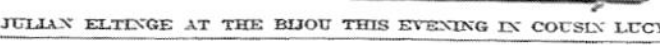
JULIAN ELTINGE AT THE BIJOU THIS EVENING IN COUSIN LUCY

Famous female impersonator in the role he takes in "Cousin Lucy," which he plays at the Wells-Bijou Sunday night.

Left: *Evansville Courier*, March 26, 1916. Drag superstar Julian Eltinge appearing in Evansville in *Cousin Lucy* at the Bijou Theater. Whole families came to see the play. *Evansville Vanderburgh Public Library*.

Right: *Evansville Daily Journal*, March 27, 1916. Double mirror image of drag performer Julian Eltinge in glowing review of his play *Cousin Lucy*, in which he played both a male and female role. *Evansville Vanderburgh Public Library*.

that Eltinge was portraying a male character dressing as a female for a purpose in the story. He would then unmask his male identity at the end of the story to come to a heterosexual pairing with an actual female character. The subterfuge was one of "purposeful drag," not an attempt to present as a female but as a male dressed as one.

Bailey would always unmask himself also and finish his stage show with a song using his own voice sans drag to reaffirm his male identity. But no one complained when either was in drag. Eltinge died in 1941, and Bailey lived to the age of seventy-seven, dying in 2015.

Evansville TV audiences could accept Milton Berle in female drag for laughs, much as they would later entertainer Flip Wilson performing as a comedic Geraldine or Bob Denver on *Gilligan's Island* occasionally dressing as a girl to fool Natives. But it was still a man in women's clothing.

Through the decades of the twentieth century, Evansville had a duality where drag was concerned: OK on TV or legitimate stage, but not in nightclubs or on the streets. The modern era witnesses mass audiences for the drag series *RuPaul's Drag Race*, which has lasted more than ten years and has a significant following locally, but when the Evansville Vanderburgh Public Library hosted a drag queen story hour at one of its suburban branches in February 2018, local residents protested loudly outside, yelling profanities at parents walking their small children in and out of the building in an unfortunate show of outrage. This was just over one hundred years after Julian Eltinge charmed the populace at the Bijou

"You've Reached the Bottom When Even Drag, Is a Drag"—*Angels in America*

Drag shows, drag queens and drag kings have a long history in Evansville. The national celebrities who appeared here in the twentieth century were one aspect of drag. The locals who performed drag in establishments in the city are another.

Not all LGBTQ people in Evansville value drag or drag performers. Not all heterosexual people value or enjoy drag. But those who do may have little idea as to the origins of local drag or the performers who were here over the decades. During a period when being homosexual was illegal and then thought of as an illness or mental aberration, LGBTQ people really owned little if anything of their own culture. There were no gay libraries or museums. We had no memorials or statues to any gay people in the parks. The one thing we owned, lock, stock and wigs, was drag.

Drag was the live entertainment of LGBTQ people, first in out-of-the-way, hidden places and then in bars and clubs that opened and closed for another fifty years. What started as perhaps crude stage shows where a DJ played a scratchy record for a performer to lip-synch to, all the way to today at Someplace Else, the gay club and also currently the Bokeh Lounge and a "boutique" bar called Mo's House in the Haynie's Corner neighborhood with electronic/computerized music and booming sound systems, drag has evolved along with the rights and freedoms LGBTQ people have worked for.

1950s and 1960s

Drag in the early years occurred in the Empire Room of the Vendome Hotel. As mentioned earlier, seventy-nine-year-old Paul C recalled approaching Bill Meyers, manager of the bar at the then-declining hotel, and offering to try to increase his bar traffic with homosexuals—a dicey proposition in 1959—by hosting drag revues with himself as the Dazzling Denise Nichols and four other drag performers for tips and cover only. Because business was slow, Meyers agreed, and shows happened on Saturday nights. There was no advertising, of course, but word of mouth spread around the city, and on show nights, Paul said, the crowd began to steadily grow.

The Greyhound bus station was across the street from the hotel, so sometimes visitors and other out-of-towners would stop in and enjoy the show. He remembered one queen who performed as Mildew Maggie and performed comedy drag.

During this interim period, the Blue Bar, which was in the basement of the Hotel Lincoln at Fifth and Main Streets, its interior painted dark blue to cover water stains left from the 1937 flood, was a popular night spot and a cruising bar for gay men very late in the evenings. Such musical luminaries as sax player Boots Randolph launched careers at the Blue Bar.

Meyers ended his relationship with the troupe in 1964. Some years later, Joe and Joan Kluemper approached Paul C about reorganizing the drag show cast and coming to the supper club they had acquired at the corner of Fulton Avenue and Division Street called Pal's Steak House. It had a big stage and good lighting and served food and cocktails. Paul went to work and organized a troupe of five queens: Denise Nichols, Vicki Starr (a blonde bombshell), Geneva Wormley (who was also a hairdresser), Peppermint Patty, Samantha and Tiffany (the only Black performer at that time). Occasionally Danny, a girlfriend of Joan's, would perform as a male, an early drag king. The Kluempers paid the queens fifty dollars per week, which they split, plus the cover and their tips.

Formerly known as Ward's Steak House and built in 1954, Pal's opened as an unofficial, official gay bar on July 4, 1968, to a packed house with its first drag revue.

Pal's Steak House became the center of drag activity for several years in the late 1960s and early 1970s. Division Street was one of the busiest thoroughfares in the city, and drivers late at night would see the queens outside the bar, smoking and chatting between shows. It became a topic of conversation, Paul said, around town. Most patrons came in through the rear entrance, as it was shielded from Division Street, though it did front onto Fulton Avenue. In those days, there was also a small hotel in the next block south, and across Fulton and south was the Union Depot, a passenger train station where the Louisville and Nashville Railroad stopped until 1971, when passenger service ended in Evansville.

Gradually, some performers left and new ones came in. Toward the end, Lori Reynolds replaced Peppermint Patty, and Bella Donna replaced Tiffany. Others came and went, but both Lori and Bella would have long drag careers in Evansville. One highlight of the Pal's era was a surprise appearance by then-famous singer/actress Leslie Uggams. Uggams was performing in Evansville at another venue and heard about the drag shows going on at Pal's. After her show, she came to the club and asked to sing with the queens, who were delighted to accommodate. It was Pal's one brush with a Broadway and Hollywood star.

Paul retired from drag in 1972. Shortly after that, Pal's closed and the building was demolished.

Another older gentleman who used the name Rachael Evans in his drag years remembered Pal's very fondly. He said at the age of eighteen, in 1972, friends with whom he was attending junior college invited him to come to Evansville. He lived in Henderson, Kentucky, where cross-dressing was illegal. He met some of the queens at Pal's who told him to dress up as a woman and tell the front doorman he was part of the show. He did so and was allowed backstage. A person could perform at eighteen but could not mingle in the bar.

He said it was a magical time for him, as he had never had any idea there were so many other gay people in the world.

> *It was like a whole new existence opened up for me, and it was wonderful. Drag was easier in the late 1960s and early 1970s because women's fashions were so artificial. Women were wearing wigs and using heavy make-up and false eyelashes, and the clothes of the time were sometimes garish. Think of Twiggy in bright floral miniskirts and bright tops. You would put on a wig, paint your face and put on a mini skirt and go to the mall and no one was the wiser.*

Many of the drag queens did rather well financially in the early days, Rachael said. "They were paid forty-five dollars per show for three nights a week. Several of them had regular day jobs as hairdressers or other work. They made an average living doing both things."

Some did not fare so well, especially the ones who also worked as sex workers on the streets when other jobs were unavailable. Four or five would live in one apartment trying to combine what incomes they could to survive in rough economic times when bar attendance was low.

Rachael's drag career was short-lived, but he remembers specifically going to the Happy Hour bar and Ramond's during the period between 1973 and

1977. The Happy Hour became the Cabaret shortly after that, and then the Swinging Door opened in 1979.

The Cabaret, at 1331 South Elliott Street, which catered more to women than gay men, had drag shows during the mid-1970s, as did the bar on Bond Street downtown called Ramond's. There were a few drag kings at the time. DJ (Donna Jean), Ronnie Russell and Mr. Buddy all did male drag in the various places that permitted it. Organizers also rented private venues to host drag as well. One place that was available and occasionally used during the mid-1970s was the Brenner Party House on Oak Hill Road near the intersection with Vogel Road.

Most of the local drag queens and kings who lived and worked in Evansville came here from very small towns in Kentucky, Illinois or other places where the claustrophobia of life in a rural place was too oppressive. As soon as they could, they came to a bigger city, where life might not have been perfect but they could be who they needed to be.

It was the summer of 1979, two years after Indiana decriminalized homosexuality, that Jim and Norma Black reopened the Swinging Door on Maryland Street. Drag performers who had been seeking a regular home found one at the Door. Lori Reynolds, Samantha, Vicki Starr (who later moved from Evansville), Gay Pauline, Miss Sunshine (who stood six feet, two inches in heels), Jeanette Wylde, Bella Donna, Geneva Wormley (who also performed as Monique Rogers) and Tori Daniels (Miss Gay Evansville 1983) all appeared in the early days at the Door.

Miss Samantha, circa 1981, winner of the Miss Gay Evansville title twice (1971 and 1981). *Samantha R.*

It was Bella who popularized a 1950s Judy Henske song about the Salvation Army. Dressed in a ragged blue dress, without her dentures and with a mop wig, Bella would bring down the house with that song. Bella was and will always be an icon in Evansville drag history. Her career spanned nearly thirty years before her death in 2011.

As the 1980s dawned, new performers would appear on the stage. Traci Dallas fled an abusive home in Shreveport, Louisiana, and came to Evansville, where she joined the drag world at the very young age of eighteen.

Left: The late Miss Gay Pauline, circa 1972, performed at the Pal's and Swinging Door. *Rachael Evans*.

Right: Miss Vicki Starr, performer at the Pal's and Swinging Door, circa 1973. *Rachael Evans*.

Traci was an early transwoman and partially transitioned over the years, living as a female. Her drag career was one of the longest in Evansville, and she was beloved by her audiences and friends. She died in poverty sadly in 2019, but her many friends raised the money for her eventual burial in a donated grave courtesy of a drag sister named Rachael Malone, a Las Vegas–style performer. The community rallied several times for performers who needed help. During the AIDS crisis, both the lesbian community and drag performers would rally to raise money for charity for AIDS causes, and the already mentioned B-Hives were a drag troupe for a short time.

One of the most popular queens was Todd Parker (1960–2003), who performed as Magnolia P. Thunderpussy (Maggie) for years at the Swinging Door and most later bars. Maggie's comedy drag was second to none, lip-

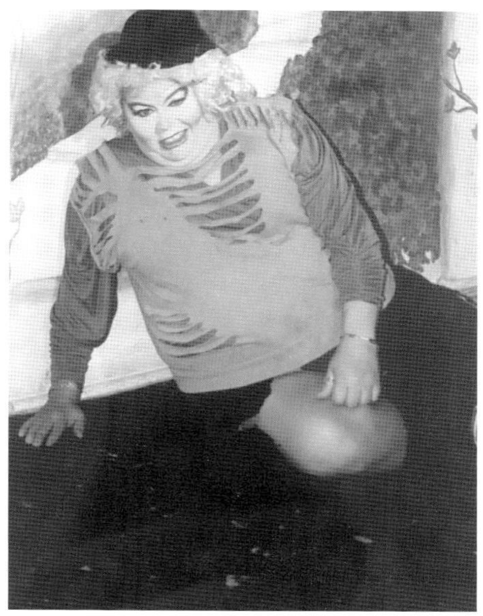

Left: Comedy drag performer Bella Donna in her signature "Salvation Army" costume, for decades a bar favorite, circa 1990. *Evy Electraa.*

Right: Bella Donna finishes her "Salvation Army" song, circa 1990. Crawling on the stage floor was common in finishing comedy numbers. *Evy Electraa.*

Las Vegas–style drag performer Rachael Malone, circa 2000. *Rachael Malone.*

Above, left: The late Magnolia P. Thunderpussy as Jackie Kennedy, circa 1985. She was a superior comedy queen for twenty years. A pageant at Someplace Else has been named for Maggie. *Evy Electraa.*

Above, right: Performance by Mama Tee, 1985 Miss Gay Evansville pageant. *Evy Electraa.*

Left: Longtime drag performer and bar owner Brittany Kimmel, circa 1995. *Bruce Crowe.*

synching songs of that generation's childhood like Connie Francis's "Where the Boys Are," which became her signature song. After Todd's passing in 2003, Someplace Else instituted a drag pageant featuring competition in both female and male impersonation in comedy to honor his memory with the Miss Maggie pageant. The showroom is named for Maggie and Ellen (Gigi's Magnolia Room; Gigi was Ellen's nickname to her grandchildren).

Some performers launched their careers in other bars. Billy Hiett, who performed as Tiffany Sex Jones, popularized a very physical performance, dancing and lip-synching at Teena Faye's. Tiffany was easily one of the most popular queens Evansville had seen to that point. Billy's younger brother Paul also occasionally performed drag as Mavis Formosa, a retired schoolteacher from Boca Raton, doing comedy songs. Both Billy and Paul passed away at young ages.

The late Terry Burnette (Mama Tee) was another classic drag performer who had a long stage career and mentored many younger queens through the years. One of the bars that opened during the later period of bar culture in Evansville was the Brickhouse, located in the urban North Side. Momma Tee specialized in ballads and giving sage advice to brokenhearted friends. The Brickhouse was co-owned by a longtime drag performer who went by the name Brittany Kimmel (Brett Ashby, who also owned a salon). Brittany Kimmel performed at many of the older clubs in the 1980s and 1990s. The Brickhouse was a welcoming place for drag kings as well. The showroom on the second floor was usually packed to the rafters on weekend nights to see such local luminaries as the late Dakota Carmichael. Momma Tee was the emcee for many shows there.

Misty Dawn (Chris Morgan) was another very popular performer. Misty was involved in a lot of charity work as well. After her very untimely passing, her husband, Charles Brennan, started the Misty Dawn Foundation, which raised money for AIDS causes and Christmas gifts for economically challenged families.

Melanie and Michelle

Two very important drag performers who were responsible for increasing the professionalism of the art in Evansville and moving shows to new venues were Melanie and Michelle Stevens, who had been performing since the early 1970s as latecomers to the Pal's Steak House scene. The pair was in drag shows at the Sho Bar and, when it folded as a gay bar, approached

Ellen Campbell about hosting drag shows on Sunday nights at her fledgling Someplace Else bar. Ellen agreed, and the two set up shop upstairs, creating a showroom space. It was not a huge room, but it served its purpose, and drag shows upstairs began in 1992. Eventually, shows became so popular they were no longer limited to Sunday nights, and Saturday and Friday night shows started taking place in short order.

An article in the *Evansville Courier and Press* from February 1995 detailed the cabaret-style drag revues at Someplace Else. It featured interviews with both Mickey and Mike Bradham (Melanie and Michelle in drag), who talked about all the background work it took to put on the shows and how much they appreciated their audiences, which, even at that early point, were at least 30 percent straight couples and bridal parties making the drinking rounds at bachelorette parties.[113]

Michelle usually emceed the shows. The pair worked tirelessly to keep drag going at the popular bar and devoted many volunteer hours to the B-Hives and any other AIDS fundraisers that came their way, donating thousands of dollars over time. One of their more notable protégés is Kendra James (nicknamed the Bath House Beauty), who recently celebrated a fiftieth birthday and twenty-fifth year performing in Evansville and the region. Although Mickey and Mike (Melanie and Michelle), now in their mid-sixties, relocated to Key West, Florida, some years ago after selling their successful business making plaster cast ornaments in Evansville, they still occasionally visit their hometown to participate in the community.

Someplace Else staff and supporters organized an early Pride event with street closures and celebrity guests in the 2006–08 timeframe. Notably, disco star Maxine Nightingale and internationally famous drag star Coco Peru appeared at the outdoor festival.

Although they were small in number for many years, after the 1990s began, drag kings became more popular forms of entertainment in the bars, especially during the time Someplace Else and the Brickhouse were coexisting. Drag kings blended in with the traditional drag queens in almost all shows and are today still well regarded in the drag culture. Beginning in 1979, Evansville became part of the statewide Drag Pageant Circuit, which culminates each year in the Miss and Mr. Gay Indiana pageant in Indianapolis.

African American drag performers were a rare commodity in the early years. Tiffany was a pioneer. Later, the late drag artist Luscious Knight grew to be a bar favorite. Coco Deville and, currently, Unique Dezire are well known in the community.

Left: Kendra James, circa 2010, is one of the longest-performing drag artists in Evansville today. Her "drag mother" was the late Jeanette Wylde. *Kendra James.*

Right: Author and drag superstar Coco Peru in appearance at a Someplace Else street party, circa 2007. *Author's collection.*

There are bar pageants that feature drag competitions for bar titles and also male and female drag competitions that enter the winners (queen and king) into the final statewide competition. The Miss Gay Indiana pageant originated in 1979. One very famous Evansville contestant, Cassidy Fellows-Sommers, was crowned Evansville's only Miss Gay Indiana in 2010 to a tumultuous cheer from Evansville friends who accompanied her to the event. Cassidy eventually moved to Indianapolis, where she still participates in state Pride events and was co–grand marshal for the first Evansville Pride Parade in 2019 along with Della Suga, a longtime activist. The author of this book was the third grand marshal that year and will always remember it.

In 2020, when the COVID-19 pandemic hit Indiana, all bars and venues were shuttered for several months. As the statewide and local shutdowns eased, Someplace Else remained closed, and the owners undertook major renovations inside and outside the club. It was the first time in nearly forty-three years there was no defined gay bar operating in the city. As venues began to reopen, the owners of the Bokeh Lounge at the Haynie's Corner neighborhood invited JD Opel (who was Evansville's only winner of Mr.

Left: Miss Gay Evansville and runners-up, 1985: Mama Tee, Traci Dallas (winner) and Miss Sunshine. All have passed away. *Bruce Crowe*.

Opposite: Drag king performer Jayden Licious, circa 2018, sponsors many community fundraising activities for children. *Author's collection*.

Gay Indiana in 2009) to organize monthly drag revues to give performers an opportunity to work and LGBTQ people a safe place to enjoy themselves in community.

JD organized the first "Dolls of the District," referencing the area's being known as the Art District, and featured artists Londyn Starz, Paris Starz, Slim Pickens and Amber Lights. Later, various guest artists were invited to participate, including longtime city favorite Coco DeVille and drag king Virgil Lee Dennison, who popularized particular country western songs. The Art District also sponsored shows at the nearby boutique-style Mo's House Bar for a Sunday brunch show. Both the Bokeh and Mo's House shows draw significant heterosexual fans as well as LGBTQ audiences. In Evansville, younger generations especially have no qualms about enjoying such events and mingling with gay/transgender neighbors. For several years, Mo's House has also been the setting for a "tea dance" LGBTQ gathering the last Sunday of each month.

A drag troupe led by king Brock Harder (who specializes in hard-hitting rock-and-roll songs) performs in independent venues and rented spaces as well, featuring kings like Xander Havoc, Jayden Licious and others. Someplace Else reopened with a huge party in September 2021, and queer life resumed as before.

Home Box Office (HBO) created a series called *We're Here* featuring *RuPaul's Drag Race* personalities who come to smaller American communities and take three ordinary citizens and transform them into drag queens, with fabulous stage shows and lighting. Evansville was chosen as one of the sites for the series, and in the summer of 2021, Evansville became part of

the show. The founder of Tri State Alliance, Yvon, married her partner at the event. One of the three local residents who "painted" for the first time was a Methodist minister, Pastor Craig Duke. Duke subsequently was released from his church for appearing on the show.

Drag has become mainstream along with the rest of LGBTQ culture. With *RuPaul's Drag Race* a TV staple, Evansville, like the rest of America, has witnessed a changed landscape in less than sixty years. Evansville's LGBTQ culture went from the closet to Main Street in that short period. Although there will always be those who look at sexuality and gender through a narrow lens of fear, bigotry and hatred, Evansville proves that humanity wins out and progress, though plodding sometimes, happens when you least expect it.

EPILOGUE

THE LGBTQ+ IN TODAY'S EVANSVILLE

Like the Family down the Street

In 2011, leaders of the Tri State Alliance began petitioning the Evansville City Council to amend its Human Relations Commission ordinance that was created in the 1940s to include sexual orientation and gender identity in local protections against discrimination in housing, employment and public accommodations. For several years, Evansville city government was reluctant to make such a change. However, in 2011, the city council, after negotiations with the Human Relations Commission attorney David Kent, agreed to put such protections in the ordinance but on a "voluntary" basis, meaning a landlord or organization that had a complaint made against it could choose either to answer the complaint or not answer it, without penalty.

The change to the ordinance was done quietly, and there was an immediate outcry from religious opponents of the ruling. In 2012, there was a change in the leadership of the Vanderburgh County commissioners, and with divided government, in order to make the ordinance truly effective, it had to also be approved by the county. Again, the Tri State Alliance organized its forces to support the measure, but this time, the opponents filled the hearing room and with biblical quotations and other "reasons" were able to argue the measure to a stalemate. It would be years before county government finally passed such a resolution.

In 2016, the ordinance was changed again, this time adding penalties for violations. In 2021, a landlord was brought before the commission for denying a housing unit to a lesbian couple, proving that the ordinance works.

The Tri-State Alliance organized an "alternative prom" in the early 2000s when two young women were denied entry into the Castle High School prom. The spring prom is now the largest attended prom event in the area, drawing both LGBTQ and heterosexual supporters and friends.

The biggest LGBTQ+ story that came out of Evansville and impacted the nation was in June 2014. U.S. District Court judge Richard Young made a historic ruling on June 24, striking down Indiana's ban on same-sex marriages. The ruling sent shockwaves through Indiana state government, and immediately, the Indiana attorney general filed an appeal to the U.S. Supreme Court, which denied the appeal, leaving Indiana as one of nineteen states in the Union that recognized same-sex marriage.

In his ruling, Judge Young wrote, "In time, Americans will look at the marriage of couples…and refer to it simply as a marriage—not a same-sex marriage. These couples, when gender and sexual orientation are taken away, are in all respects like the family down the street."

One year later almost to the day, the U.S. Supreme Court in the Obergefell decision legalized marriage equality nationwide, and LGBTQ couples in Evansville and around the nation raced to their courthouses to apply for marriage licenses. Evansville city clerk Laura Windhorst posed with several couples just days after the ruling passed after performing the first such marriages in the city.

As we have seen, Evansville has evolved over the decades in terms of its awareness, sympathy and, finally, support of its LGBTQ+ citizens. From the days when a tavern would be almost shut down for serving homosexuals, to entrapment stings and prison time for consensual sexuality, to discrimination in housing and public accommodation, Evansville has moved forward light years from the mid-twentieth century.

In 2016, the Diversity Lecture Series, an organization funded with large grants from many of the most highly valued local businesses and industries, brought to Evansville the former *Star Trek* actor George Takei, who tours the nation speaking about growing up in a Japanese American concentration camp during World War II and his experiences in Hollywood as a closeted gay actor in the 1960s and 1970s. The September lecture event was preceded by an announcement in August by the board members and Mayor Lloyd Winnecke in the atrium of the Old National Events Plaza that featured silk fabrics in a rainbow of colors cascading down onto the floor from a second-story balcony. It was something that would never have occurred just ten years earlier. Takei was warmly received, and the capacity crowd gave him several standing ovations.

As mentioned earlier, the 2019 foray of the public library system into the national trend of drag queen story hour events, where drag performers read books to children in supervised settings, drew stark comparisons in how Evansville residents saw LGBTQ+ people. Many expressed hateful, antagonistic opinions and hurled almost violent expressions of hate at their neighbors bringing kids to the suburban library for the event. Police provided heavy security, and the library was held in contempt by some. County Commissioner Cheryl Musgrave threatened to remove "county funding" but was subtly reminded the library is its own taxing district. Musgrave also suggested the library board might consider terminating the first African American woman library director in the organization's long history. Ironically, a decade earlier, Musgrave had been the first to propose including LGBTQ in the overall civil rights ordinance but was rebuffed by other leaders.

The opposite was true among many heterosexual parents who were happy for their children to learn about the diversity in people and see for themselves that it was a harmless excursion into fantasy. The breakdown in communication between the groups was never fully healed and generated reams of scary social media posts from people opposed to any mention of diversity and gender identity. Apparently, for some who undoubtedly enjoyed the aforementioned stars in drag like Jim Bailey or Milton Berle, there was revolt to the point of children hearing adults screaming profanities and slurs from people ostensibly present to "protect them."[114]

Concerns about LGBTQ youth led to the formation in 2018 of GEY (Greater Evansville Youth) at the First Presbyterian Church on SE Second Street. Jerusha van Camp, a leader in that congregation, and a committee of concerned citizens formed the drop-in group that meets regularly at the church and sponsors events for young people to meet, have supervised activities and participate in Pride activities as they can. Four blocks away at the St. Paul's Episcopal Church annex building at 301 SE First Street, there is a clothing bank called the Rainbow Jacket Project dedicated to providing clothing to transgender youth. Various groups gather in November to mark TDOR (Trans Day of Remembrance).

In terms of actual policy, although there are political officeholders who are adamant about their opposition to anything related to queer Evansville, the pervasive attitude in the city is one of support or quiet resignation that the juggernaut cannot be reversed, so live and let live.

In September 2021, Someplace Else celebrated its thirty-first anniversary under its present familial ownership and twenty-eight years as a continuously operating LGBTQ bar, making it one of the oldest in the Midwest and

New Year's Eve 2009 at Someplace Else. Shown here are the late Ellen Campbell, Brian Weir, Dustin Grant and the late Ken Gist, harpist with the local symphony, celebrating the new year. *Author's collection.*

River City Pride parade, 2022. *River City Pride/Tyler Shields.*

River City Pride festival, 2022. *River City Pride/Tyler Shields.*

the longest-operating gay establishment in Evansville's history. Still owned by Ellen Campbell's granddaughter, it represents not only the continuity of place but also the long-standing tradition of heterosexual allies who steadfastly support their queer neighbors in Evansville.

The crowds who swelled the streets at Haynie's Corner for the 2022 Pride First Friday sponsored by neighboring business owners, the multitudes who not only lined the streets but also marched in the 2022 Pride parade and attended the festival, were testimony that the community at large realizes that LGBTQ+ Evansville has come full circle.

We still have work to do here. There is still some underlying racism within the LGBTQ community that should be addressed by leaders. In many circles, ageism and transphobia prevail. Lack of a serious community conversation periodically puts us at risk of retreating to silos and cliques that keep us from moving forward. As I wrote earlier, gay politics can be brutal. But for all our faults, we have indeed come a long way.

In the June 1977 protest outside the Vanderburgh Auditorium against Anita Bryant, one of the unidentified protestors, a twenty-one-year-old college student, was quoted as saying, "The time for Evansville is at hand." He was correct; the changes were just several decades ahead. Today, he would be in his mid-sixties and, like the author of this book, nearing retirement age. If he is still in Evansville, I hope he marvels at the changes time has brought to this conservative mid-American city that I have always been proud to call home. As Ellen Campbell told the *Courier and Press* in 1995 about her commitment to the LGBTQ people in Evansville, "I think everyone should just be themselves."

NOTES

Abbreviations

EC: *Evansville Courier*
ECP: *Evansville Courier and Press*
EJ: *Evansville Journal*
EJN: *Evansville Journal-News*
EP: *Evansville Press*
SCP: *Sunday Courier and Press*

Chapter 1

1. *EP*, August 5, 1957, "The End of an Era: Infamous District in Path of Progress," 13.
2. *EV*, April 7, 1895, "His Downfall," 4.
3. *EJ*, May 26, 1895, "Among the good things…," 10.
4. *EV*, April 6, 1895, "A Scathing Verdict," 1.
5. Sodomy laws around the world, Indiana laws, August 10, 2004, George Painter, Gay and Lesbian Archives of the Pacific Northwest Inc.
6. *EJ*, February 8, 1924, "High Court Denies New Young Hearing," 5.
7. *EV*, October 19, 1948, "Two Men Face Morals Charge," 4.
8. *EP*, December 3, 1952, "Arrest of Three Men Signals Drive on Perverts," 4.
9. *EV*, December 12, 1939, "Imprisonment awaits five…," 4.

Chapter 2

10. *EP*, October 26, 1937, "Dear Dr. Crane: Question of girl's affection for other girls…," 4.
11. *EP*, September 29, 1938, "Dear Dr. Crane: Beware of Schoolgirl Crushes," 15.
12. *EP*, September 25, 1941, "Dear Dr. Crane: Youth faces stiff moral challenge…," 20.
13. *EP*, January 4, 1943, "Dear Dr. Crane: Men prefer women…," 8.
14. *EP*, July 7, 1948, "They Are No Smarter," 18.
15. *EP*, March 17, 1950, "Who Hired Them," 8.
16. *EC*, December 1, 1953, "Two Years of Treatment Made Him a Woman," 15.
17. *EC*, July 15, 1952, "Rudolph Ziemer Posts Bond in Morals Case," 7.

Chapter 3

18. *EC*, April 2, 1960, "Auto of Local Executive Murdered in 1954 Found," 1.
19. *EP*, April 2, 1960, "Reagan Case Revived by Finding of Car," 1.
20. *EC*, April 3, 1960, "Long Hunt for Killer Spurred by New Clue," 14; *EP*, April 4, 1960, "Michigan Police Completing Tests on Reagan Car," 2.
21. *EP*, September 26, 1954, "Truck Line Manager Missing," 17; *EP*, September 28, 1954, "Whereabouts of Reagan Worries Cops," 2.
22. *EC*, September 29, 1954, "Manager of Trucking Firm Missing Since Last Wednesday," 7.
23. *EC*, October 2, 1954, "Andrew Reagan Dumped in Field," 1.
24. *EP*, October 2, 1954, "Reagan Found Dead Near Henderson," 1.
25. *EP*, October 5, 1954, "No Trace of Reagan Car," 3; *EC*, November 16, 1954, "Zimmerman Joins BBI Motor Freight," 20.
26. *EC*, November 29, 1954, "Officers Continuing Murder Case Work," 5.
27. *EP*, April 5, 1960, "Reagan Case Records Going to Michigan," 13; *EC*, April 15, 1960, "New Suspect Located in Reagan Murder," 3; *EP*, April 15, 1960, "New Suspect Located in Reagan Murder," 5; *EC*, April 18, 1960, "Reagan Death Suspect Cleared Names Others," 13.
28. Kentucky State Police fulfillment of public records, accessed November 2, 2022.

Chapter 4

29. *SCP*, April 23, 1939, "Centennial to Give Operetta," 48; *EP*, February 4, 1944, "Personals," 10; *SCP*, October 12, 1947, "Clever Comedy Is Chosen for Community Players Opening," 56.
30. *EP*, November 3, 1960, "2 Held in Fatal 4 Story Plunge," 1.
31. *EC*, November 4, 1060, "Man Admits Pushing Victim at Y," 1.
32. *EC*, November 4, 1960, "Boxer Admits Knocking Burdette out Window," 1.

33. *EC*, November 5, 1960, "Grand Jury Will Meet Nov. 14th," 3; *EC*, November 11, 1960, "Murder Charge Filed in Burdette Death Case," 13.
34. *EP*, November 15, 1960, "Boxer Indicted in YMCA Murder," 8; *EP*, November 28, 1960, "Murder Charge to Be Contested," 9; *EP*, March 14, 1961, "Self-Defense Claim Hinted in Y Murder," 1; *EC*, March 15, 1961, "Claim of self-defense indicated…," 13; *EC*, March 16, 1961, "Accused Says Man Fell from Y Window," 35.
35. *EC*, March 17, 1961, "Burdette Fall Claimed Accidental," 21.
36. *EC*, March 18, 1961, "Boxer Freed in Fatal Y Plunge," 1; *EP*, March 18, 1961, "Jury Clears South Carolinian in YMCA Death of Burdette," 2.
37. *EP*, April 12, 1961, "Holcombe Jailed on Theft Count," 15; *EC*, April 13, 1961, "Holcombe Fined $25 Sent to Jail," 17.

Chapter 5

38. *EP*, July 25, 1949, "One Man Injured…in River Mishaps," 3; *EC*, November 16, 1949, "Boat Crash Victim Asks $5000," 20.
39. *EP*, March 14, 1963, "Rudy Ziemer Is Missing," 1.
40. *EP*, November 18, 1964, "Girl Tells of Night Ziemer Died," 1.
41. *EP*, March 15, 1963, "3 GI's Charged in Ziemer Case," 1; *EP*, March 19, 1963, "Soldiers Won't Testify during Ziemer Inquest," 9; *EP*, March 20, 1963, "GI's Testimony to Be Excluded," 2; *EP*, April 10, 1963, "Ziemer Jury Continues Investigation," 13.
42. *EC*, April 18, 1963, "3 GI's Indicted on Murder Charge," 1.
43. *EP*, November 16, 1964, "Ziemer Death Trial to Begin," 1.
44. *EP*, November 17, 1964, "Judge Disallows Ziemer Character Blast," "Autopsy Shows Ziemer Drowned," 1–2.
45. *EP*, November 19, 1964, "'Confession' in Ziemer Death Entered in Trial," 1.
46. *EP*, November 21, 1964, "Ziemer Defense Off in Three Directions," 1.
47. *EP*, November 22, 1964, "Ziemer defense strategy to be tested Monday…,"1.
48. *EP*, November 23, 1964, "Judge Discharges Ziemer Case Juror," 1.
49. *EC*, November 24, 1964, "Three Ex-Paratroopers Cleared in Ziemer Death," 1–2.
50. *EP*, November 24, 1964, "Not Guilty Verdict Climaxes Emotion Packed Day," 1.

Chapter 6

51. Jeanne Suhrheinrich, "Front Row Center," *EC*, April 1, 1960, 32; Bish Thompson, "Aisle Seat," *EP*, April 1, 1960, 17.
52. Jeanne Suhrheinrich, "Front Row Center," *EC*, May 5, 1962, 7.

53. Jeanne Suhrheinrich, "Advise and Consent Triumph," *EC*, October 10, 1961, 6.
54. Jeanne Suhrheinrich, "Front Row Center," *EC*, July 27, 1962, 30.
55. Jeanne Suhrheinrich"Front Row Center, " *EC*, July 4, 1970, 17.
56. William Gumberts, "Boys in the Band Is Top Entertainment," *EP*, July 4, 1970, 4.
57. Jeanne Suhrheinrich, "Front Row Center," *EC*, July 19, 1974, 11.

Chapter 7

58. Charles Schleper, "Auctioneer Here Found Bludgeoned to Death," *EP*, March 15, 1966, 1.
59. *EP*, March 16, 1966, "Suspect Held for Grand Jury," 23.
60. *EP*, March 21, 1966, "Grand Jury to Investigate Fatal Beating," 13; *EP*, July 9, 1966, "Bond $50,000 for Stutsman," 10.
61. *EP*, October 4, 1966, "Lesser Plea by Stutsman Defended by Prosecution," 13.
62. Ann Carey, "Gay Life Increases in Evansville; Worst Threat: Spread to Juveniles," *EP*, May 4, 1967, 22.
63. Herb Marynell, "The Gay Life; Female Impersonators Pose a Growing Problem…," *EP*, October 15, 1976, 18.

Chapter 8

64. *EP*, February 5, 1981, "Woman Found Dead in East Side Home," 1; Patricia Swanson and Herb Marynell, "Slain Woman Had Variety of Interests," *EP*, February 6, 1981, 1.
65. *EP*, February 10, 1981, "Convict Being Held in Slaying Called Suspect in Rapes," 1; Patrick Wathen, "Schiro to Undergo Tests to Evaluate Competence," *EC*, February 13, 1981, 19; Pam Mulkey, "Half-way House Seeks Second Chance," *EP*, February 15, 1981, 18; Patrick Wathen, "Schiro Shown as Very Very Sick," *EC*, September 4, 81, 35; Tom Wyman, "Psychologist Claims Rape Is Natural Part of Sex to Schiro," *EP*, September 11, 1981, 17; Joycelyn Winnecke, "Schiro Convicted of Rape-Murder," *SCP*, September 13, 1981, 1.

Chapter 9

66. Sherri Massa, "Clergyman Found Slain in His Car," *EP*, November 30, 1984, 1; Rod Spaw and Jari Jackson, "Priest Shot Three Times in the Head," *EC*, December 1, 1984, 1.
67. Sherri Massa, "Priest Killed Just Minutes before Body Found," *EP*, December 1, 1984, 1
68. *EP*, December 3, 1984, "Keeton Left Hotel Room before Death," 5.

69. Ron French and Cynthia Weiss, "Suspect Charged in Priest's Slaying," *SCP*, January 5, 1986, 1.
70. Barry Rose, "Arrest Ends Waiting for Minister's Family, Congregation," *EC*, January 6, 1986, 9; *EP*, January 22, 1986, "Bowers Refuses to Move Slaying Trial," 5.
71. Mike Belwood, "Suspect in Slaying of Priest Found Guilty in '79 Killing," *EC*, March 7, 1986, 19; Mike Belwood, "Bloody Fingerprint Might Be Murder Trial Key," *EC*, May 16, 1986, 17; Mike Belwood, "Collins Is Found Guilty of Killing the Rev. Keeton," *EC*, May 21, 1986, 1; *EP*, April 20, 1988, "Collins Verdict Upheld by Court," 33.
72. Thom Raithel, "Blow to Head Caused Man's Death," *EC*, September 4, 1993, 1.
73. Jim Beck, "Unsolved '93 Slaying, Russell's Death May Be Linked," *EC*, March 4, 1995, 1.
74. Patrick Wathen, "Suspect's Wife Nailed Him; She Wore 'Wire' on Day of Arrest," *EC*, March 30, 1995, 1.
75. Doug Sword, "Murder Trial Ready to Resume," *EC*, August 27, 1997, 4; Jim Beck, "Farber Sentenced to Life in Prison," *EC*, September 27, 1997, 4; Jim Beck, "Farber Again Gets Life Sentence," *EC*, January 14, 1999, B8.

Chapter 10

76. Joycelyn Winnecke, "Gays Existing in a Straight World," *SCP*, May 31, 1981, 1, 4.
77. Mike Belwood, "AIDS High-Risk Groups Get Red Cross Request to Refrain from Giving Blood," *EC*, April 5, 1983, 24.
78. Jan Aylsworth, "Social Diseases: Facts Help Dispel the Myths," *EC*, April 17, 1983, 1.
79. *EC*, May 19, 1983, "Scope of Deadly Immune Disorder Is Widening," 12.
80. *EC*, November 30, 1984, "AIDS Cases Increase 74%," 10.
81. Mike Belwood, "First AIDS Case in Area Confirmed," *EC*, February 20, 1985, 18.
82. Ron French, "Fear of AIDS Modifies Gay Sexual Habits," *SCP*, September 22, 1985, 15, 18.
83. *SCP*, September 29, 1985, "Referendum Responses," 11.
84. David Hulen, "McIntyre Urges US to Oppose Gay Sex Acts," *EC*, June 18, 1986, 8.
85. Angie Cobb, "AIDS Counseling Available Locally," *EC*, July 6, 1986, 4B; Chuck Clark, "County Wants City to Restore Fund for AIDS Educator," *EC*, August 21, 1986, 17.
86. Roberta Heiman, "Group Will Try to Deal with AIDS," *EC*, April 12, 1987, 8.
87. Ron French, "Dancer Back Home as Instructor," *SCP*, August 26, 1984, 84.

88. Bill Greer, "Evansville Dance Theater Production a Kids Affair," *EC*, June 30, 1985, 123.
89. Kim Husk, "City to Be Pilot Site for AIDS Program," *EC*, February 23, 1991, 4; Linda Negro and Roger McBain, "Tireless AIDS Fighter Loses Final Battle," *EC*, September 16, 1992, 4.
90. Terry Wells, "ACT UP to Start AIDS Campaign in Evansville," *EP*, September 1, 1992, 9.
91. *EC*, September 10, 1992, "Kmart Picketed by AIDS Group," 4.
92. Dan Armstrong and Rich Azar, "Pub Sued for Firing HIV Worker," *EP*, December 6, 1994, 9.
93. Mark Stalcup, "Former Bartender Settles Lawsuit over Firing, HIV Status," *EP*, November 1, 1995, 13; *EP*, June 25, 1998, obituary, Larry Conway, 26.
94. Polly Bigham, "AIDS Walk Organizer Honors Brother's Memory by Helping Others," *EP*, September 30, 1994, 13.
95. Carole Reins, "City Native Enthused by Cable News Effort," *EP*, July 6, 1980, 65; *EP*, July 25, 1994, obituary, G. Andrew Wright, 19.
96. Sandra Knipe, "Streetman Music to Benefit AIDS Group," *EP*, April 15, 1996, 11.
97. Matthew 25 annual report card, 2021.

Chapter 11

98. *EP*, July 13, 1954, "Everything New Except the Management," 18; *EP*, September 26, 1957, "Wards Sold to Brown and Moers," 9; *EP*, September 21, 1961, "Three Tavern Owners Innocent of Violating City Ordinance," 34; *EP*, June 7, 1968, "New Supper Club Being Built," 20; *EC*, June 29, 1971, "Injured Man Says Not Treated," 1; *EC*, June 30, 1971, "Injured Man Neglected in Jail, Relatives Say," 3.
99. *EC*, April 23, 1968, "Liquor Permit Renewal Denied."
100. *EC*, April 9, 1970, advertisement for Tony's Bar, 28; *EP*, September 15, 1973, "Door Slammed on Attacker," 1; *EP*, February 28, 1976, "Country Beat Goes On and On in Area," 4; *EC*, September 14, 1978, "City Man Seriously Wounded," 3.
101. *EP*, March 18, 1975, "Probe Delays Action on Tavern," 20.
102. *EP*, April 25, 1979, advertisement, 5.
103. Jan Aylsworth, "Alternative Lifestyle Is Basis for New Group," *SCP*, May 15, 1983, 57.
104. *EP*, January 20, 1986, "The Other Side II Bar Is Damaged by Fire," 17; Dan Armstrong, "Liquor Permit Renewed by ABC," *EP*, December 29, 1992, 16
105. Mark Kroeger, "Three-Alarm Blaze Destroys Old Mecca Bar Tavern Building," *EP*, January 25, 1982, 1; *EP*, January 26, 1982, "Owner of Tavern Tells Police of Hearing Threat," 9; *EC*, July 4, 1982, "An Era Ends," 51; *EC*, January 31,

1983, "Owner Is Charged with Burning Tavern," 15; Patrick Wathen, "Accused Arsonist Linked to Fencing Probe," *EC*, February 1, 1983, 5; *EC*, March 21, 1984, "Rager Is Found Innocent in Fire Sale," 20.

106. Roger McBain, "Gay Bar Opens in Building that Held Amanda Fenwicks," *EC*, February 7, 1992, 27.

107. Herb Marynell, "Evansville Police Discover Murder after Report of Car Crash in Kentucky," *EC*, August 28, 2000, 1; Ryan Reynolds, "Police Say Suspect Sold VCR Owned by Slain Man," *ECP*, August 29, 2000, 1; Dave Hosick, "Man Facing Murder Charges Extradited from Kentucky," *ECP*, August 30, 2000, B3; Mark Wilson, "Prosecution Says Fear of Being Seen as Gay Led to Killing," *ECP*, December 12, 2000, B1; Indiana Court of Appeals No.82A01-0103-CR-92, October 19, 2001.

108. Richard Gootee and Tori Fater, "Arrest Made in Shooting," *ECP*, July 12, 2016, 4; Richard Gootee, "Extra Charge Coming in Shooting," *ECP*, July 16, 2016, 4; Mark Wilson, "Judge: Man Not Competent to Stand Trial," *ECP*, March 21, 2017, 4.

109. Jennifer Whitson, "Hennig's New Attacks Funded by State GOP," *ECP*, October 20, 2004, 12.

110. Tom Langhorne, "Republican Criticizes Attacks on Hoy," *ECP*, June 5, 2006, 10.

Chapter 12

111. *EC*, March 26, 1916, "Julian Eltinge in New Show 'Cousin Lucy,'" 26; *EJN*, March 26, 1916, "Julian Eltinge Is at Wells-Bijou Sunday," 22; *EC*, July 3, 1977, advertisement, 87.

112. Rick Barter, "Jim Bailey and friends…," *SCP*, July 10, 1977, 3; John Penn, "Female Illusions Saved Him," *EP*, July 13, 1977, 3.

113. Segann March, "Official Threatens EVPL Funding over Drag Story Hour," *EC*, January 31, 2019, 1.

Epilogue

114. Michael Doyle and Segann March, "Drag Queen Story Hour Draws Many Fans, Foes," *EC*, February 24, 2019, 2; Tori Fater, "Councilman Elpers Reports Threats to Police," *EC*, February 26, 2019, 2; March, "Official Threatens EVPL Funding."

ABOUT THE AUTHOR

Kelley Matthew Coures was born in Evansville and graduated from the University of Southern Indiana. He has served as the executive director of the Department of Metro Development in the city of Evansville since 2014. In 2011, he received the Sadelle Berger Civil Rights Award from the Mayors Human Relations Commission for work in the LGBTQ community. He served on the board of the AIDS Resource Group in the 1990s, and in 2012, Leadership Evansville presented him the Social Service Award. He has been married to Justin Allan Coures since 2017, and together they struggle to parent two spoiled French bulldogs.